Afternoons with the Devil

Growing Up Catholic in a Border Town

Marty Gervais

LIBRARY AND ARCHIVES CANADA CATALOGUING IN PUBLICATION

Gervais, C. H. (Charles Henry), 1946-
Afternoons with the devil : growing up Catholic in a border town / Marty Gervais.

ISBN 978-0-88962-919-6

1. Gervais, C. H. (Charles Henry), 1946-. 2. Catholics--Ontario--Windsor--Biography. 3. Windsor (Ont.)--Biography. 4. Poets, Canadian (English)--20th century--Biography. 5. Journalists--Canada--Biography. I. Title.

PS8563.E7Z53 2010 C811'.54 C2010-906390-2

Published by Mosaic Press, offices and warehouse at 1252 Speers Road, Units 1 and 2, Oakville, Ontario, L6L 5N9, Canada and Mosaic Press, PMB 145, 4500 Witmer Industrial Estates, Niagara Falls, NY, 14305-1386, U.S.A.

Printed and Bound in Canada.
ISBN 978-0-88962-919-6

We acknowledge the financial support of the Government of Canada through the Canada Book Fund (CBF) for this project.

Nous reconnaissons l'aide financière du gouvernement du Canada par l'entremise du Fonds du livre du Canada (FLC) pour ce projet.

Canadian Heritage Patrimoine canadien

Canada

And the Ontario Media Development Coorporation (OMDC)

Mosaic Press in Canada:
1252 Speers Road, Units 1 & 2
Oakville, Ontario
L6L 5N9
Phone/Fax: 905-825-2130
info@mosaic-press.com

www.mosaic-press.com

Mosaic Press in U.S.A.:
4500 Witmer Industrial Estates
PMB 145, Niagara Falls, NY
14305-1386
info@mosaic-press.com

Afternoons with the Devil

Growing Up Catholic in a Border Town

Marty Gervais

mosaic press

Acknowledgements

Assistance on writing this book was provided in part by the Ontario Arts Council Writers' Reserve program through recommendations from *Descant*, *Biblioasis* and *Palimpsest Press*.

Jasmine Elliott, my assistant at the University of Windsor, helped me through the summer of 2010 in assembling and organizing much of this book. Help, too, was provided by Amber Pinsonneault, Sarah St. Pierre, and by Jordenne Rachelle, Susie Heinrichs and Kate Hargreaves for finding all those typos.

I am also indebted for the encouragement shown by Howard Aster of Mosaic Press, to my wife, Donna, and the clear advice and levelheaded editing from my friend and poet John B. Lee.

Some pieces from this book arose out of columns I had done for the Windsor Star, as well as from another book *Tearing Into A Summer Day*. In all cases, these were rewritten and expanded.

The names of some characters and locations in this book may have been changed, as have certain physical characteristics and other descriptive details. Some of the events and characters are also composites of several individual events or persons.

Table of Contents

For my grandchildren, Calder, Cicely and the new kid, and for Julien and Sebastien...

Things That Counted

There were only a few things you had to keep clear in those days—*Who had the highest batting average? Who had the lowest ERA? Who won the Stanley Cup last year?*

I had little trouble with any of these, but year after year the nuns stumped me with the second question in the Baltimore Catechism: *Who is God?*

My brother Billy pulled me aside one day and told me not to worry—the truth was, he said, I don't think they know either—that's why they keep asking.

Bless Me Father

That spring in Rome, I telephoned a Trappist monk from the Abbey of Gethsemani and invited him for lunch. We arranged to meet at the Obelisk in the centre of Vatican Square. I arrived earlier than expected and frowned when I spotted the meandering queue into the St. Peter's. I filed into line anyway. Moments later, I was roaming about inside. I still had time to kill, but when I spied a bank of confessionals in full operation, all in different languages, with one specifically labeled ENGLISH, I thought, why not?—I haven't been in years. But the impulse was more casual, something to do at the Vatican, like running the bases at Wrigley Field or posing in front of the Eiffel Tower.

I slipped behind the dark curtain and the panel slid open. The voice in the darkness was distinctly American. I felt pretty well at ease.

"Bless me, Father, for I have sinned," I started, paused then realized I had to specify how long it had been since my last confession. So, I said honestly, "It's been a while since my last confession. . ."

The priest cut me off: "A while? How long?"

"Well...several years..." I vacillated.

"Several? Well, a couple of years would be two. Is it two? More than two? If it's more than two, then it's several, but that could be ten, or fifteen or twenty?"

I panicked, and blurted out a decisive "Twelve."

Why twelve? I don't know. It's a number. The twelve apostles of Christ? The twelve tribes of Israel? The twelve astrological signs? Maybe I was thinking of how the modern clock is divided into two groups of twelve. Our ancient measuring systems are also based on that number: a dozen, a gross which is twelve times twelve, a shilling which is twelve pence, and a foot which is twelve inches. I don't know why I told this priest it was twelve.

"So, it's twelve," he said. I sensed he knew I made that up.

The priest wasn't finished with me. He was preparing to embark on a "physical" of my soul. I was about to be administered a spiritual prostate exam.

"Have you ever doubted the teachings of Holy Mother Church? In other words, have you taken part in non-Catholic worship? Gone to Protestant churches, taken communion there, and practiced any superstition, like checking your horoscope? Going to fortune tellers?" he started.

"Well, I'm a Libra...Is that bad?"

"Do you believe in that?" he asked.

"In astrology?" I asked. "I mean, it's fun. I read it in the paper every day, and it kinda sums up what's happening... for the day... It's just fun—it doesn't mean anything."

"So, slapping God in the face by following astrology is fun?"

"No," I said defensively. "What I mean is, I don't believe in astrology. I think...I think...it's nonsense. It's fun to watch others rely upon it, is what I mean, I guess."

"So, perhaps you relish in the ignorance of others?" the priest persisted.

But he didn't wait for my reply. He had already pressed on to Commandment number two: "Do you swear? Do you take the name of the Lord Thy God in vain when you are frustrated, angry, upset? Have you maligned priests in any way, said terrible and wrongful things about their calling?"

"Never!" I said emphatically. I glanced at my watch, and needed to bolt from this confessional box, and meet my friend. "Never, never, never!"

"Really?" the priest probed.

"Yup, never! I have never, ever sworn. I might've said

something like, 'jeez' but I never finished off that word, so I don't know if that counts and whenever I really wanted to say damn! I said 'darn!"

Moving on: "Have you missed Mass through your own fault? Fallen asleep at Mass? Worked on Sundays? Shopped on Sundays?"

"Shopped on Sundays?" I interrupted. "Well, sure, I mean, who doesn't? I mean, the malls are open. It's not illegal."

"So you have?" the priest asked.

"Sure, I mean, is that a sin?"

And so it went, all the way through the Ten Commandments. This American priest bullying me, probing my soul, wanting to know if I had quarreled with anyone, neglected my children, set a bad example for them, engaged in gossip, taken pleasure in others' misfortune, been jealous, disrespectful to my parents ("They're dead," I said, thanking my lucky stars I didn't have to lie about that one).

He wanted to know if I ever denied my spouse her marriage rights (what does that mean? I thought, but told him straight away I had never denied her marriage rights. Not ever!) Then of course he got to the best part: adultery, fornication, sinning with someone of the same sex, and sex with animals. Had I ever watched porno films? Looked at indecent photos? Masturbated? Had lustful desires?

"No, no, no."

Then he wanted to know if I had killed anyone, and I blurted out: "You mean, in the past twelve years?"

Why would I say that? It implied somehow that I was absolved of murder in my last confession twelve years ago.

"No, not ever!" I said.

"Have you ever lied?"

"Never!"

"Never?" he asked incredulously.

"Not that I know of," I conceded. "I mean, sure, probably, yes, maybe. I am sure I might've. I mean, who doesn't? From time to time that is...No, but I don't lie from time to time. I just lie, and then I lie again, but it isn't often...but it wasn't or hasn't been like that in twelve years. Not ever. But before, I did."

I had said too much. There was silence.

"Anything else?" the priest asked.

"Can't think of anything," I said. "You pretty well covered it all...and thank you." Why I said, 'thank you' I'm not sure. Nobody says that in confession. And for all this bother, my penance was two Our Fathers, three Hail Marys, and one Glory Be.

This brings me to this—growing up Catholic. This brings me to my story. The writers of another book, *Growing Up Catholic*, published in 1985, described a Catholic perfectly when they wrote that they believed "in things they have never seen, felt, or heard, and they believe most deeply in things they have never been able to figure out."

True enough. We do. We go on faith, and when it doesn't make sense, we call it "a mystery." As a Catholic boy, I didn't question my religion. We were told never to read the Bible and so we didn't . We were told never to eat meat on Friday, so we didn't . We were advised to go to confession once a week, and so we did. We also attended Mass every Sunday, as well as every one of the Holy Days of Obligation. We also considered the priest to be the only educated man in the community and if we needed guidance on any question at all, we knocked on his door.

Obviously things have gone awry in the church. Now Holy Mother Church is being pestered with questions of a different nature. Now the man in the Roman collar isn't trusted.

That brings me back to the man in the confessional box in Rome. Why didn't I interrupt his spiritual grilling, and tell him maybe it's time he starts listening?

Instead, I walked back out into Vatican Square to meet my friend.

Mr. Know-It-All

The first day of school: St. Thomas School in Riverside, Ontario. September 1951. My two-day-old haircut was slicked down. I wore a hand-me-down, cotton, white shirt, and new pants a few sizes too big—but I'd grow into them—bought at Sam's in Detroit. I carried a school bag with stiff, bright, yellow pencils, a couple of scribblers, an eraser, and a note from my mother ingratiating herself with the nuns.

"Tell them you want to sit up at the front," my mother exhorted me.

"Why?" I asked.

"Look, you have a problem in paying attention," she argued.

"But...but I've never been in a class!" I said, a little bewildered. After all, this was my first day ever.

"What I'm saying," my mother explained, "is you're different. You're not like your brothers who do pay attention. You're simply different."

"Huh?" I said lamely.

"Never mind, tell the sister you want to sit at the front."

I was five. I was going to be six in October. I walked to the school—it was only across the street. I walked up to the first nun I spotted in the yard and formally proclaimed,

"I'm supposed to sit at the front."

She towered over me. Her hands were clasped behind her back like a drill sergeant. She glared at me with steely blue eyes.

"You're already telling us what to do?" she asked.

"Huh?" I said.

"I'm saying it's your first day here, and you're already telling us how to run things," the nun said.

I skulked away, desperately in search of my older brother, but the school principal, Sister Mary of Perpetual Help, who we later called "Sister Mary of Perpetual Hell," was already on the steps of the school, and clanging the bell. We filed into school. Naturally, I wound up in the wrong classroom. I had trailed after a group of others into one across the hall from where I should've been. A kindly old nun then led me to the grade one class where I was met with a scolding look from the same sister I had met in the yard. My luck!

"So, we have Mr. Know-It-All who hasn't got a clue where to go!" she declared.

I made my way to the only empty seat in the classroom—a seat at the very back. And when I went to sit down, I tried to make room for my schoolbag, and in lifting it up, my elbow accidentally toppled over the school globe on to the floor. I then found myself stupidly chasing this huge, metal ball across the room. Laughter broke out from all quarters.

Within four seconds, this incensed nun—Sister Bartholomew—was breathing fire down my back: "So, Mr. Know-It-All, you're making quite an impression on your first day!"

I began to stutter.

"Spit it out!" she said.

I stammered, "I'm sor –"

"Maybe you need to go to your seat!"

"I have a note to give you," I continued boldly.

"A note?"

"Yes, my mother wants me at the front of the class." I said.

"She does, does she?"

"Yes –"

Sister Bartholomew cut me off: "So that's where you get this know-it-all attitude. From your dear mother! I guess she wants to tell me how to run my class. I guess maybe she should be teaching this class!"

I was five. I didn't have a clue why she was angry with me—I had never seen her before in my life. I was shaking in my boots. My hair stiffened on my head. I was perspiring uncontrollably. I didn't know what to do next. Finally, I went over to the corner of the classroom and picked up the globe. I stared at it for what seemed an eternity. I made a wish that I could jump into that blue ocean and swim a thousand miles away from this nun. I also imagined myself walking ashore in a country that had no nuns at all, and being greeted by strangers who smiled at me, and liked me immediately.

"Now what are you going to do?" this nun demanded, breaking my reverie.

My hands trembled as I carefully placed this colourful globe into her grasp. I feared the worst. Finally, I stammered with surprising wit: "Here's your world!"

Royal Tour of Windsor

I STRUGGLED ALL ONE AFTERNOON at St. Thomas in making a paper Union Jack flag that I could wave when Princess Elizabeth toured the city that fall of 1951. We were told by the nuns to take these paper Union Jacks home and fasten them to a narrow stick, or at least something we could hold on to, so we could wave them as the princess and the Duke of Edinburgh passed by.

We were also reminded that the twenty-year-old Princess Elizabeth was an Anglican and she couldn't help it, because somewhere in the distant past, this overweight bearded Henry VIII didn't listen to the Pope and finally had to turn his whole country against Catholics.

And so while it was fine to wave our Union Jacks in the streets, we should also offer a silent prayer for the princess in hopes that she might turn Catholic.

I was six. I didn't understand any of this. All I knew was she was going straight to hell, because she wasn't Catholic. I mean, all Protestants were headed there. That's what Sister Bartholomew told us.

Still, I searched through the garage for something suitable for my Union Jack, but my oldest brother agreed he'd take care of it before morning. The next day before running off to school, I couldn't find the Union Jack. I was in a panic, when suddenly I spotted it. My red, white, and blue flag was tucked neatly in the bottom of the budgie cage. Covered in seeds. My mother stammered, "I thought it was a rough copy!"

Bow Ties

THE BOW TIES WERE KEPT in a shoebox on the top shelf of a cupboard in my father's bedroom. He'd stopped wearing them in 1959. He had worn them almost from that time in 1926, when he rode the train south that winter from Cobalt. He moved to Albert Road in Ford City. He wore it to the interview at the Canadian Motor Lamp. He got a job on the line making headlamps, but got fired a week later. Too skinny, they said. But my dad begged the floor manager to keep him on, and with some reluctance, the company assigned him to work with the women. Soon he was the foreman. Much later, he was promoted to plant manager and superintendent. Like the others, he wore a white shirt every day. My mother ironed them every night. And he wore a bow tie. He also sported a Clark Gable mustache, and he started smoking.

When I was five, my father dressed Billy and I in white shirts, and he clipped a bow tie to each of our collars, brushed back our hair like his, straight back, no part, and we drove off to church like that. Each Sunday. We wanted to be like him. When we grew up, and started our own families, and accidentally caught sight of ourselves in a store window or mirror, we recognized that look, that sullenness of my father all over again. We hated that. It was everything we had hoped for as children, but now as grown men, we needed something else, our own soul, not his.

Finding the bow ties was like looking at old school pictures of ourselves. We wore those ties on Sundays, all day long, and by nightfall we tossed them across the dining room at one another. I never saw the point of these ties. They seemed like fake ties, half ties, a gesture, a half-hearted nod in deference to ties. When I scan that photo of Billy and me sitting together, these bow ties look like misplaced eyebrows clipped to our shirts.

Marty Gervais

Sin

After I wrote in the *Windsor Star* about the experience of Catholic confession in the 1950s, I received some fascinating letters. One, in particular, caught my attention because it referred to an expression the nuns always used, something they called "the near occasion of sin." It was mentioned in the same breath as "Indulgences."

I heard that for the first time in grade one at St. Thomas. I was barely six.

I did not understand it. It was far too convoluted. I also felt a little under the gun when Sister Bartholomew, a squat-looking nun, kept twisting her beads nervously around her cold, veined hands as she paced at the front of the class and asked if I knew what "the near occasion of sin" meant.

I slowly shook my head—concentrating solely upon the word "occasion"—then murmured, "a party?"

Sister Bartholomew glared at the class, and at me in particular: "Yes, you're right—it's a party with the Devil! It's a roaring good time with Beelzebub! It's a romp with Lucifer! It's a dance with the most beautiful angel that God ever created, but when he thought he was better than God, and thought he was God then God banished him to the fires of hell. . .That's where everyone of you will be going if you sin—you'll spend a roaring good time in blazing fire!"

We were stunned.

"Do you know what sin is?" Sister Bartholomew asked another classmate.

"Does it mean being bad?" she said.

"Have you been bad?" the nun asked.

"Yes—I don't always listen to my mother."

That's when we learned all about sin and the arithmetic behind Indulgences and purgatory. We had already heard about purgatory, and knew limbo because a baby down the street died last winter, and everyone whispered that the child was going to limbo because it had not been baptized. Eventually with a lot of prayers, this baby would reach heaven, but not just yet. It was not the baby's fault, but it also was not God's either. That was my mother's reasoning.

Purgatory was another matter. Venial sins, or smaller sins, could land you in that place. It wouldn't be anywhere as bad as hell, but it would definitely be uncomfortable. It would definitely be hot, and the food wouldn't be good, and there wouldn't be TV, no Disney, no sports or pop, and certainly no chocolate.

This is where the nuns got into the arithmetic of purgatory. Lying to your mother could send you into exile for a couple of hundred thousand years. The only way around it was to stockpile what the church provided as "Indulgences," or special prayers, or acts of kindness that would somehow lessen the punishment for your sins. And a single day in purgatory, the nuns warned us, would feel like a thousand years of anguish. But if you recited your prayers before meals for one full week without fail, you could win back twenty years. If you made the sign of the cross, that might erase another 150 days, and if you performed this with holy water, there was a bonus. And if you served Mass on Sundays, as well as one day during the week, and you did that for seven straight days, you could deduct six years from your sentence.

My brother figured he'd scored the big one when he traded a stack of holy cards, including five different St. Francis of Assisi images, for a card that contained a miniscule bone chip from St. Gerard. This relic was worth at least a thousand days off time spent in purgatory. I stared at it for a long time and when I told my brother it looked like a fingernail, he beat me up.

In any case, if you could find a thread from the Virgin Mary's veil, chips of wood from the cross on which Christ died, or bits of bone or flesh from the bodies of martyrs then you were in the money when it came to indulgences. You had the potential of releasing a lot of souls.

At six, or eight, or nine, the concept of indulgences sounded a lot like the game of Monopoly and being handed a get-out-of jail card. But you didn't dare mention that to the nuns. All we came away with was the reality that there were two kinds of indulgences: *plenary* and *partial*. Plenary was what you wanted—it wiped away everything. But it was difficult getting those. You pretty well had to know someone who knew someone. Like the Pope. Partial indulgences were easy enough to acquire—you could help an old lady by carrying her groceries or run errands for a neighbour—but remember, these only wiped away a part of your sin. Things get muddy in trying to determine how many innumerable acts of kindness translated into making this imposed sentence shorter in purgatory. I was terrible at arithmetic and always got my hands whacked by the nuns whenever I counted on my fingers. I finally resigned myself to the futile reality that if I landed up there, I planned on staying. After all, I reasoned, if I wound up getting that far, for sure, I wasn't going to hell.

Another One In Hell

It silenced us all one July afternoon when we learned my older brother Bud's best friend was killed after a truck backed up and crushed him at a loading dock in Windsor. He had gotten this job right out of high school.

This was a Monday morning when I read about it in the paper. I pored over the photograph of the truck, and read the story several times, and I don't know why—maybe it's because I couldn't believe it. It had just been yesterday when he was at our house, laughing with a wooden basket brimming with apples in his arms as he came through the kitchen door. He was with Bud. And my mom asked where they had gotten the apples. That's when he told us the story of how he climbed over a farmer's fence with my brother and raided an orchard. The two heaped the truck of his '49 Ford with Macintosh apples. They then peeled off down the road. They were laughing so hard in the car that when my brother started whipping apples at his buddy he tried to duck, and his car swerved off on the shoulder of the country road, and nearly went into a ditch.

Then there I was on the Monday, staring at the photograph in the paper of the truck. Only yesterday he was sitting in the basement yammering about how he'd filched those apples right under the unsuspecting face of the farmer. That's when it occurred to me this was Sunday. Sunday afternoon. Confessions were Saturday. And my brother's pal—and Bud—had broken the eighth Commandment. *Thou shalt not steal.* There was no chance of him ever getting to confession. He'd pretty well have had to wait till next Saturday.

I couldn't keep my eyes off the graduation photograph in the paper. I studied his face and the dark shadows around his eyes. There was no chance of him ever repenting for that sin with a priest. When Billy, my other brother, settled down beside me on the floor, I told him what I was thinking, and he nodded knowingly like the expert on everything. We both gaped at one another in that instant: Bud's friend must have gone straight to hell—he must have been the first one we knew of from the neighbhourhood.

In Search of Santa

I WAS EIGHT, and on my knees, poring over the newspaper spread out over the living room floor.

"Mom!" I yelled. "There's a guy in Windsor, Ontario, who has six hundred fingers! His name is Harry Vexler!"

"What!" my mother shot back. "What do you mean? Six hundred fingers?"

It was Christmas Eve, and a full page of the *Windsor Daily Star* displayed photographs of all the people who worked for Harry Vexler, who once owned a department store on Ottawa Street.

"It says it right there, Mom!"

In one glance, my mom explained to me how Harry Vexler was merely thanking all the people who made his business successful over the past year. The figure "six hundred" referred to the staff, associates, and suppliers who had helped him to that success. It was merely a Christmas greeting.

I recall that year for another reason. It was the year the kids in our neighbourhood in Riverside decided there was no Santa Claus. We had it all figured out. From the year before, someone caught their mom or dad placing presents—allegedly from Santa Claus—under the tree.

Word spread. A few days before Christmas, we huddled in the schoolyard.

"There's no such thing as Santa!" my cousin Dennis told us bluntly.

"What do you mean?" I asked incredulously.

"Just what I said: No Santa!"

I walked off, feeling heartbroken, certain he was lying.

There had to be a Santa. Our parents were so cheap, they wouldn't think of buying us all this stuff. They didn't at any other time of the year. Why start now?

It wasn't so unusual for me to wonder about such things. It also wasn't unusual for me to ask questions. Only a few months before, I had cornered my mom in the kitchen and asked her about where babies came from. She ignored me as she went about cleaning. I persisted. She finally gave up and sat me down, and over the next ten minutes ran down the facts of life in the most convoluted manner, addressing subjects of gestation, menstruation, ovaries, and sperm. I was so overwhelmed with detail I made for the fridge, cut myself a piece of pie and escaped out the back door.

But here it was, Christmas approaching, and word had hit the schoolyard—no Santa.

I decided to ask my teacher. A young nun. She told me, "Jesus is Santa!"

"What?" I asked, wrinkling my brow.

"Yes, Jesus in the manger!"

I didn't get it. I joined my friends in the schoolyard. I decided I had better go to a higher authority. The principal. I lobbied Sister Mary of Perpetual Help. She had to know. She sat me down and asked, "Who told you there was no Santa!"

"Dennis!"

"Your cousin?" she said. "I'll have to have him in here to explain himself!"

I could envision the cloakroom strapping and no explanation being given to Dennis. I felt demoralized. So, I wrote Santa in those big jagged letters with a red crayon and sent it to the North Pole.

Dear Santa, My cousin Dennis says there's no Santa. He says it's our parents who buy all the gifts! Is this true?

Marty

My older brother, Billy, looked over my shoulder and told me, "That's dumb. If there is no Santa, why are you writing to him?"

I was so mad I threw a hockey puck at him. He pursued me down the street, swearing he was going to rip up the letter. But I escaped and managed to drop the letter into the mailbox. Two weeks passed. And one day when I came in from school, my mom said, "There's a letter from Santa!"

The next day, only two days before Christmas, I proudly took the letter to school. The kids gathered around me, endeavouring to read it.

It read:

Dear Marty—Yes there is a Santa.

That's who I am! It's also true, your parents put out the gifts, and go to the stores and get them...But they get them with special gift certificates I give them every year and you can use them at any store in the land.

Merry Christmas.

Santa.

To this day, I don't know for sure who sent the letter. Maybe it was Billy. Maybe it was Dennis. Maybe it was Santa.

Marty Gervais

HAPPY TRAILS, ROY

HE WAS MY HERO for about a month. I sat in front of the black and white television in the basement room on Prado Place, and slurped up Sugar Corn Pops, and watched.

Roy Rogers.

The cowboy with the polyester face and boots to match.

It was the Cold War. The Centre Theatre in Riverside was the spot to be. Home of Westerns. And my mother—suspicious of the effects of this savage death and mayhem swirling on our young minds—would dispatch us to the movies with a stern warning to stop by Our Lady of Guadalupe on our way home and go to confession.

The church in those days regularly tacked the Legion of Decency's ratings to its bulletin board. *Rio Bravo* fared poorly.

Those Saturday afternoons after the movies, we'd whisper in the dark confessional box, and tell the priest we had disobeyed our parents, lied, cheated on arithmetic tests, entertained "bad thoughts," and had just been to see John Ford's *The Searchers* (1956) starring John Wayne.

"Was it good?" the priest inquired.

"The movie, Father?"

"Yes."

"Oh, yeah, it was terrific!"

"Lots of killing?"

"Oh, yeah!"

"Knifings?"

"Yes Father!"

"Did you count how many died?"

"No, Father, but a lot."

"Good...Now son, would you say three Our Fathers, three Hail Marys..."

This was the golden era of the cowboy. We were all cowboys then and now we had the unofficial dispensation, or imprimatur, from this Catholic priest who seemed to want to kill as much as we did.

So desperate to have chaps, we swiped the oil cloths from the kitchen table—much to my mother's chagrin—and cut them up, turned them inside out, and strapped them to our legs.

Like Roy Rogers, and Gene Autry, and the Lone Ranger, who often climbed atop buildings to pursue their enemies, we'd use my neighbourhood cousin's low-frame house with a tarred roof.

Once thinking my bully cousin Dennis was hiding in the bathroom, my brother Billy lowered me upside down to peek in the window. To my horror, my uncle was sitting on the can and reading the *Windsor Daily Star*. As my shadow fell over his paper, he spotted me. I remember little of that, except my brother failing to haul me back up fast enough. And my heart was pounding all the way home.

In the midst of all this, Roy Rogers was the good guy. The ambassador of goodwill for cowboys. Fair-minded, considerate, well spoken. The Wayne Gretzky of cowboys. He had even written the Ten Commandments for cowboys. I maintained he was better than Zorro, The Cisco Kid, Hopalong Cassidy, and John Wayne. We played them all. And I played Roy Rogers. At least, until my brother Billy got to me. He convinced me Roy Rogers was a fake cowboy. Too prissy, clean, and unruffled. Besides he never shot anybody and never got his hands dirty.

"What's with Dale Evans? Lipstick? And all that singing?" he'd taunt.

"Have you ever heard John Wayne suddenly break into song on his horse? C'mon!"

I was eight. I believed my brother. I believed everything he told me. He was the authority. He knew more than anybody.

Still I harboured a secret desire to join the Roy Rogers Fan Club. I didn't. I fell into line and acknowledged John Wayne as the real king of the cowboys.

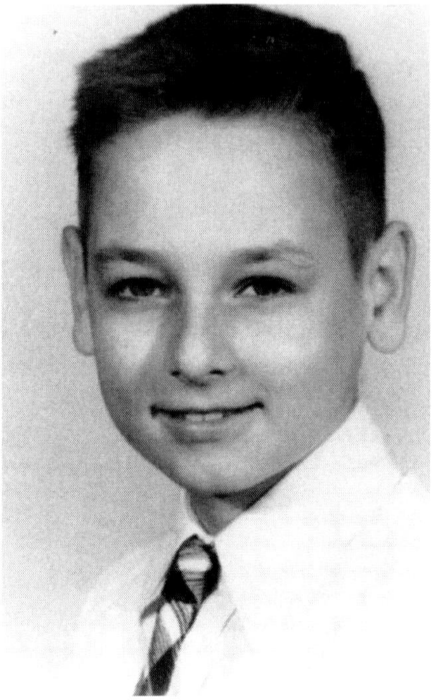

The movies then were the poetry of our lives. So uncomplicated. Kill the bad guys. Something basic and simple. Unfettered like Shakespearean trickery playing up that tension of good and evil. And we'd scurry through open fields around Prado to hide in construction sites. With our silver-painted pistols glinting in the summer sun as we ducked behind sand piles. We got Vue-Masters for Christmas that showed slides of the Cisco Kid.

We'd dutifully eat the cereals endorsed by cowboys, like Roy Rogers plugging Sugar Corn Pops because "Sugar Pops Are Tops!" We indulged ourselves in everything that was western. Kerchiefs tied around our necks, holsters, sheriff's badge, and spurs on our running shoes. We continued this until we became smitten with Elvis, then danced in our stocking feet in the basement listening to Dick Clark and American Bandstand.

Watching westerns didn't spawn a generation of killers and bank robbers. Maybe it's because of Roy Rogers and what he said at the end of each show: "Goodbye, good luck and may the good Lord take a liking to you!"

The Baltimore Catechism

I HAD TROUBLE WITH THE Baltimore Catechism. The first question was pretty easy, or so I thought. *Who Made The World?* Sister Bartholomew glared down the aisle at me, and selected me even though I had lowered my head, and was studiously scratching at the markings, and ink-stains on the wooden desk top.

I wanted to say it was God.

But when I looked up, I spied the picture of Pius XII on the wall. I pointed at him.

"I think he did? Right?"

Sister Bartholomew tapped a wooden yardstick against the broad palm of her left hand, cocked her head to one side, rolled her eyes back, and sighed: "God did, my son! God! Not the Holy Father though he is a blessed man! But no, he did not make the world! God made him. God made me. God made you!"

I knew that—why did I point to the Pope? What got into me? I must've looked befuddled, because Sister Bartholomew then ventured along the aisle and was idling above me. The wimple and rimless spectacles pressed tightly against her squarish face. I spotted tissue tucked up into her voluminous sleeves. But all of my attention gravitated to a few straggly hairs that hung from her chin as she mouthed her question: "You seem confused. Do you not understand?"

I looked away and muttered something. She then leaned down and asked me to spit it out. I blurted out, "But who made God? I mean...you can't come from nothing, can you?"

I was now banished to the cloakroom where I slumped on

the floor staring up at coats and umbrellas.

Meanwhile, Sister Bartholomew's sharp voice prattled on to the rest of the grade one class about how God was the creator of heaven and Earth, and of all things, and that we, his children, were composed of body and soul, and made in His image and likeness.

So I look like God? I thought. I was puzzled. Eugene, and Billy don't look like each other, and they don't look at all like me either, and Patricia doesn't. I mean, she's pretty and has nice, long braids, and she's from Holland, but I don't look like her, and she certainly doesn't look like me, but we're all supposed to look like God? So shouldn't we all look the same?

I knew I would be in even more trouble if I returned to the classroom and asked Sister Bartholomew about that. Best I sit and listen. I did. I sat there till recess. Finally Sister Bartholomew unlocked the dark, wooden door to the cloakroom and she towered over me. I couldn't help but stare at those hard, black oxfords. They seemed so huge.

"Well," she said.

"I'm sorry," I said, then trying to redeem myself went on to elaborate: "Now, I know who God is. He looks like me, doesn't he?"

With that, I was left in the cloakroom for the rest of the day.

I Confess To Almighty...

WITH THE CATHOLIC CHURCH encouraging its faithful to return to that practice of confession, it brought me back to those Saturday afternoons when we'd file into line at Our Lady of Guadalupe Church and tell Father Mooney our sins.

The one topping the list was disobeying my parents.

As I have said earlier, my mom—eager for peace and quiet—sent us to the matinees at the Centre Theatre, and afterwards, we'd dutifully toddle across the street to the church, and queue up for confession.

The lines there were endless.

When it was finally our turn, we'd slip past the velvet curtain and overhear the mumbling of some penitent on the other side—most likely a pal, or a brother. Then the screen would slide open to reveal the outline of the bald pate of Father Mooney in the dim light and we'd start in. Same old stuff every week. Same old penance—three Our Fathers, two Hail Marys, and one Glory Be.

At seven we didn't know what sin was. Our transgressions were narrowly limited: lying and not listening to our parents. Deep down, we knew our dad's punishment was worse than God's, so we rarely veered far off the mark. Beyond that, we had no idea what sinning was. That led to some interesting confessions and funny scenarios.

Once, my older brother Bill mischievously advised me to confess that I had committed adultery. I had no idea what that was, but he assured me I had done it. So, I tallied up the list of sins that one Saturday and confessed I had disobeyed my parents four times, lied once to my teacher, and that I used "bad words" in anger.

"Anything else?" Father Mooney asked.

That's when I let slip that I had committed adultery seventeen times—a figure my brother had calculated.

"That's fine. . .Three Our Fathers, two Hail Marys, one Glory be."

Well, that couldn't have been such a bad thing, I thought.

My brother had a good laugh when I told him, but at ten, he didn't have a clue what adultery was either. "It's something Mom and Dad do," he mused.

This was the era of Gunsmoke and Ozzie and Harriet. Confession was a big thing. We inventoried our sins. Kept crib-notes on our hands. Once a buddy of mine couldn't make out what he had written, so he lit a match inside the confessional box to get a better look, causing the priest to bolt from the confessional figuring the church was going to go up in flames.

Another time, I was kneeling in the confessional box when an older gentleman—not realizing I was already in there—stepped in. Most likely a bit senile. When he knelt down, huffing like an old horse, I was virtually pinned against the wall. Strangely, he never noticed me. Meanwhile, I didn't utter a word. I was too scared. I was seven. Finally when the priest opened the panel, the man started in with his sins, but so did I. Bedlam resulted. Naturally, I was blamed for this prank.

Much later as a teenager, I went to confession at a northern Ontario boarding school and told the priest about "having sex" with a teenage girl and he calmly offered me this analogy: "My dear boy, sex is like onions...I can eat onions all day long. I can slice them up and put them on my sandwiches, or put them into soup, or fry them up with my potatoes, or eat them raw. I love onions. But I know if I do that, eating onions will offend other people. I will have trouble with gas and bad breath."

"Sex is like that. If you have sex all the time, it can be offensive, but it is most offensive to God."

"Son, there's a time and place for onions—in moderation—and there is a time and place for sex, and that's in marriage."

It made sense, to a point. But now every time I have sex, I think of onions.

From my youngest years, however, the best was Saturday afternoon when I was maybe eight. I had just come from watching a John Wayne movie and filed into line behind my brother. The lines snaked down the aisles. I was desperate to go to the bathroom, but wouldn't leave the queue. And the priests were taking forever.

Finally my brother slipped into the confessional and I followed but on the other side. I could hear Bill rattling off his sins, much the same a mine. He was taking such a long time and now I was squirming because my bladder was ready to burst.

Father Mooney finally slid open the panel. I began, "Bless me, Father, for I have ..." but in that moment, I couldn't hold it anymore. I felt that generous warm, wet rush into my pants—I was peeing uncontrollably. I started again, "Bless me, Father, for I have just peed in this confessional!" The priest—straining to make sense of what I was saying—asked gravely, "How many times have you done this, my son?" To which I responded in tears rolling down my cheeks, "I am doing it right now Father!"

I then fled the confessional, racing all the way home, holding my wet pants and believing in divine certainty that I was headed straight to the restrooms of hell.

Visiting The Dead

THE DAY WILL BE SPENT visiting the dead. That was the way my mother put it when she slipped a starched white shirt on me and affixed a bow tie to the collar. I wore my brother's hand-me-down pants and a pair of shiny, black shoes two sizes too big. I was nine. I was ready to meet the dead.

I went outside that morning and waited beside my father's green 1953 Plymouth with the "Flow-Thru" fenders. It was parked under the blooming lilac trees. My buddy from across the street wandered over and asked why I was all dressed up and I told him I was going to see some dead uncles.

I had never seen a corpse before, except on television. I was pretty excited by the prospect. He told me he had seen one last winter when his uncle died. It was nothing special. He had thought before going to the funeral home and seeing him, that his uncle's eyes might be gaping open, like the cattle-rustlers on Gunsmoke, when they lay dead in the street in Dodge City at the hands of the righteous Marshall Matt Dillon. I didn't know what to expect. As I say, this was in the mid-1950s and it was not uncommon for morticians to cart their embalming equipment to the homes of the deceased and make all the arrangements for visitations right there.

And that was the case when we set out to drive to Stoney Point where two uncles, or cousins of my mother, had died. Both the same day. They weren't at funeral homes—they were laid out in the parlours of their farmhouses.

I was thinking about this when I was at a funeral home earlier this week and how common back then for funerals to be held in homes. I read once about a New York funeral director who conducted most of his business this way, but finally had to expand to include funerals at the funeral home. As a matter of fact, he put on an addition to accommodate this. But after constructing this new wing, he discovered its flat roof often would freeze over and his children used it as a skating rink. And one day when he was carrying a casket out the front doors, he spotted his daughters doing "figure eights" on the roof and realized how unseemly this was for the family of the deceased.

Now, for that moment when we drove to Stoney Point and made our way from one farmhouse to the other, we climbed the back stairs to those sprawling kitchens with the wood stoves and saw the men standing around in the kitchens smoking and drinking. The women, dressed in black, were in the parlour comforting the widow who also wore black. The blinds on the windows were pulled down and candles were lit to lend a peaceful ambience to the darkened room. That was the custom.

I didn't know the men who had died. I had never met them. We were there to pay our respects. It strikes me now that this was part of our education, our growth. We became acquainted with death early on. We became familiar with the mystery and emotion of it though we may never have understood it and maybe we don't now. As the years went on—opportunistic as this sounds—I became an altar boy and funerals were a chance to earn a few bucks. The priest would telephone my home and ask if I could serve at a funeral mass. Inevitably, someone would slip me two dollars for helping out.

But as a boy of nine standing in front of a casket in the farmhouse parlour, off the kitchen, where the priest mingled with the men before inviting everyone to gather for prayers, I saw my family in a different light. Years later I would file into line at downtown funeral homes for the deaths of other family members and friends, but by contrast it seemed more like an appointment, more formal, less familiar.

Sure maybe as a kid I thought for the first time in my life that I, too, would die some day—that I could. But in farmhouses tucked away on the concession roads of Essex County, somehow having the funeral there made such realities easier. Or maybe that's the way I remembered it.

Personal Histories

When a lawyer for the Sisters of St. Joseph in November 2006 went to Windsor City Council to argue there was no historical significance to site of the old convent at the foot of George Avenue and Riverside Drive, I mused, "You don't know. You weren't there in the 1950s."

Let me share this little piece of history. True, nothing "significant" in the grand scheme of things. Nothing that would change the world. Nothing that would lower our taxes. Nothing that would end poverty or bring about world peace.

Let me tell you this story. I had turned nine in late fall,1955, when a new sister arrived at St. Thomas to replace the nun who came every Thursday to teach us piano. My brother Bill and I had been registered by my mother. She insisted all five of her sons take piano lessons. We had it easy with this nun. We'd thrash and pound away at the piano keys. We'd steal a glance at the sister and notice how her head had drooped and suddenly she was fast asleep, snoring ever so softly. I gave her an elbow once and she revived, and exclaimed with glee, "Oh...lovely!" Then she'd affix a coloured star to the page of my piano book.

Soon Sister St. James came into my life. She replaced the retiring elderly nun and telephoned the parents of prospective students who had been taking piano lessons to announce she would be holding "auditions" because she was recruiting only the cream of the crop. Lessons now would be conducted at the convent, not the school.

My mother immediately extolled our virtues to the new sister, claiming we were "the best." Sister St. James—eager to hear us—put us at the head of the line. Bill went first and scrambled up the staircase to the school's tiny music room at. I stood outside the door and could hear the nun swatting his hands as he struggled through the C scale like someone traversing a minefield. I could hear Bill's painful yelping.

Ten minutes later Bill opened the door. His face was ashen.

"Your turn!" he droned.

I wanted to bolt for the nearest exit. The next ten minutes were hell.

The sister then telephoned my mother to say we were "the worst" she'd ever encountered. She rejected us. My mother—ever persistent—resorted to groveling, but also talked of "miracles" and promised novenas, and special prayers. Finally Sister St. James acquiesced and agreed to teach one of us. I was the chosen one. Not because I was better.

Sister St. James had told my mom, "There's no point in teaching these sons of yours—they're both so horrible! You pick!"

That's when I became familiar with the convent. For the next three years, every Saturday morning, I'd ride that lumbering bus to that sprawling, grand old building facing the Detroit River.

I dreaded those first months. The dour-faced sister never once complimented me. She could easily detect if I hadn't practiced. She also never once rewarded me with any coloured stars. I worked like a slave, toiling every spare moment, turning down friends who tried to lure me away to play road hockey. I couldn't practice enough. It became an obsession. I didn't care if I was failing arithmetic and history. I had no other choice.

Soon I was performing perfect Bach minuets.

A moment that stands out is the Saturday the Royal Conservatory of Music examiner tested me. When I was finished, I fell short by one mark of first class honours,which would have qualified me for that tiny pin. After the examiner departed, Sister St. James sat down beside me on the piano bench. She wore that same stern face. I expected she was disappointed in my performance. I was wrong.

"I listened to you," she explained. "I was outside the door. He (the examiner) was wrong. You should have had first class honours. You should have this pin." With that, she handed me the tiny pin given to honours students—the pin I would've been given had the examiner scored me one mark higher.

"You earned it," she said gruffly, "and I want you to have it—you are the best student I have."

It's a moment I have never forgotten.

Certainly, nothing significant in the annals of the order of the Sisters of St. Joseph. One nun and one small boy. Their history. In this moment in time.

When my family moved north, my mother found a kindly, older woman to teach me piano. She swooned over a Chopin piece I knew was rusty by Sister St. James's standards. I felt embarrassed.

"Oh, that's so good!" she exclaimed. I knew it wasn't. I could tell. As I stepped through the door to return home, she handed me a selection of sweets wrapped in a delicate doily.

"What's this?" I asked alarmed.

"A little reward."

The nuns had never done anything like this. I thanked her and trotted down the pathway from her house and around the corner. That's when I pitched the candy into the nearby hedges. I knew that for the sisters, the study of music was serious. Playing was an art, a passion. The true reward was indulging in its magic.

Face To Face And Bubble Gum and Chocolate Bars

I never really thought I'd see her again. I was twelve when my family moved away from Windsor. She had told me I resembled her long-lost son. She showered me with favours whenever I stopped in at Baker's Dairy Bar on Wyandotte Street, down the street from where I lived. She gave me an extra scoop of ice cream, chocolate bars, bubble gum, anything I desired. She was like a favourite Aunt.

But I never truly knew anything about her. It may be because I truly never listened to her. I always wished I had. And so I wrote a story about her for the *Windsor Star*—of course never mentioning her name, because I didn't know it. I simply mentioned there had been this kindly woman from my childhood who showered me with candy.

Then this four-line email arrived, like a dove on my shoulder, revealing that she was the woman in the paper, that she was still very much alive, that she was eighty-six and she'd love to see me again. I sat by the phone all morning waiting to telephone her and feeling terribly nervous. I hadn't seen her in fifty years. I turned over and over those last moments in my mind when my parents dropped me by Baker's to say goodbye in 1958. That morning, she hugged me and handed me five dollars.

That was so long ago. I had figured she was long dead. And while my life has taken numerous turns since then, the story of this remarkably kind-hearted woman with red hair who believed I was the spitting image of her son, never left my thoughts. It is a story I have told countless times. It is a story

I tell people when I meet them at Baker's for breakfast. It is a story I have told my children, and my wife a thousand times.

Now finally, here I was, driving to her house in the east end. Her name is Mary. She asked that I not reveal her last name. I didn't know what to expect when I rang the doorbell. I didn't have to think about it for long, because when this lively woman opened the door, she cupped my face in her hands, and kissed me on the cheek. She said she had waited a lifetime for this moment.

Believe me, she still has red hair, and green eyes, and a smile that opens doors and windows everywhere. That's how deep of an impression she made upon me. Somehow I buried its magic, tucked it away, yet I never failed to stop telling people about her.

As it turns out, Mary, too, never ceased relating that same story about the boy from Riverside who looked so much like her son. Then ten years ago when she spotted my photograph with this column, and read about me living in Riverside, and growing up Catholic, she turned to her husband, Don, and said, "That's the boy!"

She knew everything about me, that I was an altar boy, had gone to Our Lady of Guadalupe, that my brother had been in the seminary, and that I had toyed with the idea of being a priest. She knew everything about me, possibly because I told her all this stuff. I had that insatiable desire to tell people things. It used to get me into trouble. My father would say I should hold back. I never did. It's what would later define me, along with that curiosity that showed no boundaries.

Anyway, there we were, this Catholic boy, now a man, wondering about Mary.

She told me, "I wanted to call you so many times, but never did."

Now we were face to face.

Mary was thirty-eight when I knew her. Slim. Good looking. A single mother making ends meet in the midst of a recession. Getting thirty-five dollars a week from an ex-husband before finally landing a job at Baker's. The grimmest period in her life. That might explain why the day I strolled into her store was the one bright spot in her life.

"That first day you came into Baker's, I thought you were my son. Same age and fair hair. I was so certain, I looked out the window to see if my ex-husband's car was there dropping you off. You were so shy, so polite. There were days when I'd look for you, because it made me feel good. Then when you left, I was so sad."

The son I resembled was living with an aunt. He had had rheumatic fever, and a heart murmur, and the hospital had wanted to keep him. However, her ex-husband's sister, who didn't have children of her own, offered to keep him at home and did.

"You thought he had died because I told you he wasn't with us anymore," she explained. As it turned out, with the

custody battle over the children (she has three others) and his illness, Mary never got to raise that son. He's healthy now and lives in Windsor.

"You don't know how many times I have told this story to people," she said. "I don't think anyone believed me."

Sunday Visitor

We all wanted to be priests. Five sons. Five altar boys. All raised on the border. We assisted at Mass, memorized Latin, marched in May Day parades, made novenas, went on retreats, and most likely recited a million rosaries. No wonder makeshift altars sprang up throughout the house. Billy and I routinely said Mass in an upstairs bedroom.

We also inveigled and coached a younger sister to make routine confessions to us.

So carried away we became at "playing Mass," we swiped another oil cloth from the kitchen table—just as we had done for making cowboy chaps—and we turned it inside out, painted a broad cross on it, and transformed it into a liturgical vestment. We all wanted to be priests. We fashioned chalices from tin foil, and cut up Wonder Bread into circled wafers. We swiped incense from the church, and set it ablaze in our bedroom chapel, and in moonlit darkness of our room said Mass. We wanted to be priests.

At Our Lady of Guadalupe, when we presented the starched lavabo towels, and the narrowed, glass containers of water at Mass, to Father Dill, we marveled at how white his hands were. We all wanted to be priests. Five boys.

One brother nearly made it to the priesthood, but dropped out of the seminary. Another went to work for the bank. Another became a cop, but later became a deacon. Another became a security guard. And I started writing for a newspaper. The one we thought would make it ceased going to Mass altogether. Each Sunday after Mass, he'd comb through the *Sunday Visitor* and pen countless letters to monastic orders telling them how sincere he was about joining. And my father—all one hot summer, 1956—slumped in a dining room chair, and wearily fended off Resurrectionists, Capushions, Franciscans, Redemptiorists, Basilians, and Christian Brothers. One by one, he sadly confessed how his son had absolutely no desire for religious life, how the boy fanned his hair into a ducktail, drove a hot rod, stayed out all night, and might soon set the record for failing grade twelve more times than any high school student in the province.

May Day Parades

I should have expected Harry Annan strolling into the newspaper office in 1999, and flipping open an album of the May Day parades—it was the fiftieth anniversary of its inception. As this former parade organizer from the '50s and '60s spoke, that time flooded over me. That's when religion was a part of everything we did—part of family life, schooling, and recreation.

I had always wondered what happened to the May Day Parade and why it suddenly collapsed in 1966 after eighteen consecutive years. It once boasted of being the largest of May Day parades in North America. Some 55,000 turned out to

that event—then an ecumenical celebration involving the orthodox churches and the Anglican Church.

"We really thought we'd go on forever," said Annan.

"Then they, (the priests) lowered the boom."

One local priest single-handedly scuttled the event, persuading others it was outmoded. It was never held again. Devotion to the Blessed Virgin was passé, seemingly paganistic. Certainly out of sync with the modern church that had bigger concerns—birth control, the changeover from the Latin Mass, and the falling enrollment at seminaries. Much later would come sexual abuse and scandal.

I have good memories of that earlier era. We had a sense of purpose then. Every boy in my neighbourhood wanted to be a priest. It never happened in my family. Five boys, all of us altar boys, and all winding up with mortgages, and wives. Though one finally became a deacon and that would have warmed my mother's heart. She had expected at least one would go into the priesthood. She was on her knees every night, praying for each one of us. She told us we were all equal in her prayers. She gave us all the same attention.

Anyway, there we were in the '50s being schooled in Latin, and marching in May Day parades, inching our way up Ouellette Avenue to Jackson Park's band shell. Bishop Cody presided at the podium reviewing us like Dwight Eisenhower surveying Allied troops. We were soldiers. Members of the Blue Army, a religious group born out of the Fatima revelations right before Elvis Presley took America by storm. Somehow we knew this was our answer to the May Day parades in Moscow that flexed the Russian might. Somehow we knew this was our answer to Communism, the Godless society of the Bolsheviks. This was the Cold War. We were children of McCarthyism. Neighbours constructed bomb shelters. And the piercing air raid sirens without fail every Saturday shattered our Saturday afternoon calm. The parade was our Catholic way of thumbing our noses at the influence and tyranny of the people who hated God.

I was ten, so what did I know? I wasn't questioning anything. All these fresh-faced kids marching up the street, the glow of Detroit towering above, the nurses in smart, white uniforms, and caps, lolling on the lawn at Hotel Dieu. The patients in wheelchairs waving. The balloons. And single file, we made our way, incense trailing in the air.

But it wasn't all perfect. When I walked in my first May Day, it was night. I was sick from having stuffed myself with chocolate bars. Walking didn't help. As I made my way up the street, I glanced over at my older brother and told him I had a stomach ache. He told me I would embarrass the parish if I dropped out of line. So I persevered. Suddenly, the moment we made our way past the band shell occupied by the Knights of Columbus with their swords, and plumed hats, the priests, donning black birettas, and the bishop wielding a crozier, I started retching. It was like a scene out of the 1973 *The Exorcist.* Projectile vomiting. The starched, white surplice of an altar boy in front of me was where the first volley landed, like being hit by winter slush from a passing car.

The next landed on the shoes of one of the organizers. I was bawling my eyes out. The last thing I recall was my brother breaking ranks, like a gelding out of the gate and vanishing into the crowd. The next thing was my father driving home. Gritting his teeth, saying nothing.

I expected a Blue Army court martial.

Angels With Dirty Faces

HUNDREDS OF ALTAR BOYS scrambled on to trains from all over the London Diocese to make their way to London to hear this soft-spoken, Italian priest encourage them to start thinking about being priests.

A nice idea. Bishop Cody's idea.

This story is really Father Gerald Quenneville's, as told to me by a friend. How in the late '50s that youthful, good-looking priest arrived at the Windsor train station to meet up with these boys from his parish. The kids waited on the platform—all dressed in starched, white surplices, and frayed black cassocks. The look on the faces of their mothers immediately telegraphed the message that something was awry. Their eyes didn't speak of forlorn farewell. Their smiles were more self-satisfied smirks. They knew their kids.

And what folly for these men of the church—with absolutely no experience over the care of children—to believe they could maintain order among hundreds of healthy, active kids on a train ride to London without a woman's help.

Good luck. And God forgive them.

By Belle River, the neatly packaged lunches the moms had made for their angelic boys had been pillaged. By Tilbury, all the water in the train had been drained and the toilets were out of order. By St. Thomas, the train crew was ready for mutiny, as altar boys mimicked hundred-yard dashes up and down the cars.

"A big mistake," mouthed a silent Father Quenneville, whom I imagined sunk his head into his hands.

The idea upon arrival was to have the kids parade up

Richmond to St. Peter's Basilica on Dufferin. About a fifteen to twenty-minute march. You might assume it ought to have been orderly, pious, joyous. Instead swarms of kids broke lines, and bolted for the shops, raiding comic book stores, candy counters, dimestore windows.

The next morning the *London Free Press* flashed a front page picture of one altar boy, minus the halo, but with a fat cigar stuck in his mouth.

Finally, upon reaching their destination, the altar boys filed into lines after a lot of venomous and frustrated coaxing from many of the priests who were now having serious doubts about their own vocation. They assembled at the cathedral, standing on the newly mown lawn, straining to hear this kindly old priest whose voice carried maybe only two or three rows.

It didn't take long for this momentary decorum to erupt in bedlam as boys began to engage in a war of tossing mounds of grass clippings at one another. The boys also yanked down the collars of other unsuspecting altar boys in front of them and jammed grass down their backsides.

This was not a moment of glory for Holy Mother Church. This was the work of the Devil. And oh my Lord, a collective moan among the priests, was heard: There would be confessions droning on all over the diocese from altar boys. Every confession the same. *Bless me Father, for I have sinned...I misbehaved in front of a holy priest from Rome...*

An event these diocesan priests would have preferred to forget.

It wasn't long before the altar boys were herded back on to the trains. This time, Father Quenneville—brows furrowed and his dark piercing eyes flashing in anger—positioned himself at the front of the train car. He removed his belt then warned the boys in no uncertain terms that if any one of them stepped out of line, he'd strap them.

When the kids arrived back in Windsor, they rushed into the arms of their moms and pointed back at Father Quenneville, reporting how he had threatened to strap them. That didn't sit well with the moms. But Father Quenneville didn't wait around to answer questions. Instead, he hastily retreated like a defeated Confederate soldier to the rectory, and, as my friend reported, Father Quenneville threw himself down on the floor in the living room. A fellow priest stood over him.

"What's wrong?" he implored.

"Never mind," replied a beaten Father Quenneville. "Get me a drink. Fast."

Marty Gervais

The Strap

I WAS SPEAKING WITH A FORMER NUN recently and the conversation came around to when the leather strap ruled the day in classrooms. It's inconceivable now to think this even existed. But imagine your son or daughter returning home from school, and coming clean about acting up in class, and how the teacher wielded a leather strap, and began to strike their bare hands. Such an occurrence today in schools would lead to firings and charges of assault.

When I was growing up, it was normal. *Spare the rod, spoil the child.* If you thought you got any sympathy from your parents, think again. My father's line was steady and consistent: "You probably deserved it!"

It made me cast back to Grade One when Sister Bartholomew, irritated by my conduct, grabbed me by the scruff of the neck and hauled me off into the cloak room where I was given the strap. I was barely six. My crime? I had been squirming about from a girl tickling the backs of my legs while I was reading to the class.

Having come from a family of four older brothers where problems were settled by intimidation and fists, I wheeled around and smacked this girl across the face. Truthfully, I believed that I was in my rights to do so, but the nun thought otherwise. She must have felt badly about it though, because when I was departing school later that day, she motioned me over and handed me a card with Pope Pius XII's picture on it.

As time went on, it occurred to me that girls rarely—if ever—received the strap. It also occurred to me how much they relished watching us emerge from the cloakroom holding our stinging, reddened hands. They always snickered and giggled, secretly sensing they, in many cases, were the cause of our punishments.

One woman told me with overbearing self-satisfaction that her role in the classroom was to fetch the strap whenever the teacher had to punish someone.

From my days at St. Thomas, there was one boy who mischievously tied a ribbon to a girl's long, braided, pony tail and loosely attached this to a limp, dead mouse he had found in the schoolyard. The instant she rose to recite some memorized passage to the class the rodent was catapulted into the air due to her futile and frustrated efforts to detach herself from the otherwise lifeless mouse as she wheeled about wildly in the classroom.

And who can forget sitting hushed in our seats, awaiting the cries from the cloakroom? The punished usually marched off to that room full of bravado, but when the strapped student returned to his seats, he was hurt, contrite, and humbled, hiding his burning hands.

And all the tricks to counteract the pain did no good. Older students advised us to rub chalk on our hands to dull the sting, but the nuns were wise to this and ordered us to spit in our hands. They knew this would intensify the pain.

One classmate—so fearful of the strap—yanked his hand away just as the teacher was about to strike him. She wound up hitting herself.

One teacher kept a detailed log on the number of times we were punished in an effort to pile more humiliation upon us. For example, if you received the strap a second time, she would make you peel chewed gum off the underside of school desks then tape this to your nose.

I distinctly remember slouching in my seat for the rest of the day with discarded teeth-dented gum—hard as a nugget—stuck to the end of my nose.

Another time our parish priest strolled into the classroom right when this harried teacher was strapping a classmate. The look on her face is something I will never forget. Embarrassed, she blurted out: "Father, thou shalt beat him with the rod... and shalt deliver his soul from hell...Isn't that right, Father?"

The priest was frozen in bewilderment, not knowing if he should offer approval. But everyone was staring at the boy—the toughest in the class. His smile ran right up the side of his face to his forehead. He was having the last laugh.

Prayers and Nun's Hair

The last day of school. Those five words still resonate with me all these years later. They still send an electric charge through me, because the last day meant the beginning of summer. The start of all good things.

That last week of classes in 1958 prior to my family moving away from Windsor comes to mind. The temperature hung around the mid-eighties and the humidity flattened us. We clamoured around the one decent, shady tree in the yard at St. Thomas and traded baseball cards. I was in grade six and hoping to pass despite my poor behaviour and low marks in everything except art.

If I was lucky enough to catch sight of my best friend's mother, Joan, whose property line hugged the schoolyard, I'd run over to her—on the side reserved for the girls—and she'd hand me a bottle of Vernor's. That's when I'd catch Sister Aloysius scowling at me as she promenaded through the blur of skipping ropes and running kids. I'd chug down the Vernor's and feel it burn in my chest. It felt good. And Joan would retreat along the walk at the back of her house, never looking behind.

"What did I tell you about this?" came the pointed question from Sister Aloysius. I'd shrug. Such an infraction meant remaining after school to clean the brushes, and organize the chalk, and wash down the blackboards. But on those final June days, it was futile trying to teach us anything. We were too hot. Our minds, fried. Our desire for summer, too great. Our desire to lounge in a round rubberized kiddy pool, the only thing on our minds. It didn't matter that we would slump in it, our gangly legs and arms—so incredibly white from the winter—flopped over the sides. It cooled us down. Life was sweet. Except for school. We wanted out. We were prisoners counting down the days for release. It was a matter of time and we resigned ourselves to that. If there were any plots afoot, they were to break into the office and change our marks.

Meanwhile my mom confessed she was praying for me. She knelt before the statue of St. Jude on the dresser every night and prayed to this "saint of hopeless causes." I was among that select group. It was only after she died that I picked up that statue in her bedroom and realized that in all those years she'd been praying to St. Jude, she never realized the icon on her dresser was not of him, but St. Joseph. No matter.

I can't forget June 1958. There had been talk of our family moving away. And two days before school ended, a freakish and bouncing tornado had ripped through the area, devastating much of Lasalle. It was that typical tornado weather with the sky twisting into a pea green. The nuns at St. Thomas told us how the Lasalle Catholic school kids sprawled on the floors of their classrooms praying the rosary while this twister rocked the area, knocking down hydro and telephone poles, and ripping through farm sheds, and lifting up cars, and tossing them like mere toys.

My last memory of that school was a stifling hot day and running an errand up the dark, wooden stairs to the principal's room. The door was shut to the office and so I quietly pushed it ajar, and was about ready to announce myself, and deliver this message when to my horror I spied one of the younger nuns, Sister Ignatius seated with her back to me. I could see her short wavy blonde hair. She had removed the starched headband and starched face linens, probably because of the heat.

The sight of that nun without this head covering stayed with me for days. It was something we were never privy to.

It didn't seem right.

Like everybody else, I had figured nuns were bald.

The End of Summer

When I was growing up, the last day of summer was the day before going back to school. It had nothing to do with the autumnal equinox. It was the end of holidays and the neighbourhood around Prado would gather in the schoolyard at St. Thomas and we'd build a bonfire from discarded wooden crates from the Canadian Motor Lamp on Seminole.

The flames would lick like the fiery tongues of hell deep into the far off night.

And we'd race about the schoolyard, stumbling over our parents' lawn chairs, laughing and running. We'd play hide-and-seek and howl like crazed wolves at the night sky. And when our parents called us for something to eat, we'd scramble around the wooden tables, and snatch metal coat hangers to skewer hot dogs, and marshmallows, and plunge them into the fire.

I swear my cousin Dennis downed twenty-two hot dogs that night. His belly bulged out like a pregnancy and we stood in the murky darkness examining it. I swear.

The men—all sporting Clark Gable mustaches and slicked-back hair—drank beer, and smoked, and talked about jobs, the Cold War, Eisenhower, Sputnik, Rocky Marciano, Mickey Mantle.

The women huddled on lawn chairs planning the start up of the euchre club.

Life in the neighbourhood. A picture out of *Leave It To Beaver*. And Frank Sinatra's voice, singing *Anything Goes*, from a nearby car radio.

It was the end of summer.

We marvelled at the night sky, a brilliant inky-blue. Classes were back tomorrow. The very schoolyard we were in was where we would start again, in earnest, in anticipation to make things right, somehow to reinvent ourselves. At home in our bedrooms, our satchels were already stuffed with notebooks, new yellow HB pencils, metal geometry sets, and brand new pocket *Highroads* dictionaries. Our school clothes and spanking new black and white running shoes rested on our dressers. And somehow we innocently believed all the mistakes, and classroom transgressions, and bad marks from the year before would be wiped out and forgiven. We'd all be back in our seats, all geniuses, all class pets. By October, we knew it wouldn't be so. We already anticipated the inevitable parental question: "What happened?" And we had already rehearsed our reply: "My teacher hates me!" We knew she did.

But that night before the start of school, cavorting in the darkness of the schoolyard, we felt a part of some secret pagan feast, certain there were no watchful eyes from the Sisters of St. Joseph. We knew Sister Mary of Perpetual Help—God bless her soul—was nowhere in sight. And so, we scaled the building, borrowing a ladder from a neighbour's garage and once on the roof, we ran along its tarred flatness and whipped marbles at automobiles on Thompson Boulevard. We also taunted passersby who'd search frantically about under the street lights wondering where these voices originated and then we'd hide near the roof's air vents, giggling mischievously.

It's there we practised new swear words, mouthing them like someone learning a new language.

Freedom's night. A night of thumbing our noses at authority. A night when we listened only to our own reckless impulses. A night when we could be kids and do things only kids could dream about. A night when there'd always be a parent to offer a boy a swig of OV.

And we'd tug at our father's arm and plead, "C'mon dad, let me have a taste!" Maybe we pushed the limits. Like other kids, we didn't play Old Maid and Go Fish—we learned poker from a friend's mom across the street. Maybe it was wrong. Maybe it was wrong to rifle change from our dad's wool pant pockets and maybe it wasn't OK to set a friend's fort on fire. But we weren't bad kids. We knew our limits. We knew something about loyalty, about not squealing on someone else. We knew what it meant to hurt someone's feelings with a lie. We knew right from wrong, but we got away with murder.

The Parent-Teacher Interview

THE PARENT-TEACHER INTERVIEW. That time of the year. A part of our culture, what defines us. The reality check on our kids. It makes us think about the future (What will he ever do in life?). We think about the past (Where did we go wrong?). We think about the present (Can we afford a tutor?). We move into the parent-teacher interview each year at this time, just before Christmas. We move into it like an awkward dance. We don't always know the steps. We don't always know the music. We don't even know the partner.

Parents go dutifully into elementary schools and high schools to find out the inevitable. If our children are in those junior grades, we sit on miniature chairs that might well have been used by Baby Bear in the story of *The Three Bears*. We stare blankly at pasted up cut-outs from magazines. We stare at jagged printing. And read words spelled "dint" for "didn't." We then get a look at the desks of our kids. And after four children who have gone through the system, I'm no longer surprised to find these desks jammed with loose papers, and books, and on occasion, an untouched peanut butter sandwich from October.

Then we're escorted to the back of the class to load up on all the coats, and hats, and boots forgotten by our kid over the past three weeks. This is school in the 21st century. The report card. The interview. The anxiety.

Once I was warned that our son didn't understand the basic function of a noun and a verb. My wife was distraught. "Oh yeah," I challenged her, "What about those colourful words he scrawled in a fit of frustration and anger on the wall of his bedroom about us, his mom and dad? Look, there's the noun! There's the verb. And there's the object!'

"Like it or not, no matter what he's saying about us, dear, that's a complete sentence! I think he's making progress! "

Things weren't any different for me when I was growing up. Once, I sat in a storeroom cleaning brushes. After a while, the principal stopped by because she had noticed the door was shut, and could see flashing, and flickering coming from under the door. She opened the door in a panic, and found me with an old clickety-clack movie projector casually watching films I had pulled from some steel canisters, and wound on to the reels. Fortunately for me, she wasn't angry. Instead, she smiled and remarked, "Well some of my teachers don't even know how to operate these machines!"

But I was always in trouble. Mostly it was because I failed to pay attention. My grade five report from St. Thomas stated that I spent too much time "daydreaming." My marks were the worst in the class. I was the class clown. I wasn't just making faces—I was drawing faces and once was sent home for doing a cartoon of Pope Pius XII and sarcastically writing underneath it: "Pope Bias XII."

This barb annoyed the Sisters of St. Joseph who ordered me to pray the rosary on my knees in front of the statue of the Blessed Mother all the next morning. I doubt that it helped. That was 1956. That was the year my mom and dad made me accompany them to the parent-teacher interview. Unheard of in those days. I sat meekly across from Sister Mary of Perpetual Help. My father, with brows furrowed, started: "What are we going to do about this boy?"

It's true, my marks were abominable. It's true, I acted up. It's true, I disrupted the class.

I sat there, trying anxiously to look away. Then I heard the sister: "It looks like there's no hope for this boy, doesn't it? But look at this!"

And she rose, and went to her desk, and came back holding a watercolour of a fishermen on a dock and the Detroit skyline rising in the background. The water and sky were a deep azure blue. "Now, see, this is the same boy who can't do long division—but he sure can draw, he can paint, he can see pictures."

"Don't worry about him."

Meatless Fridays

If the United Nations has its way, "meatless Fridays" may be back in vogue. Someone brought to my attention a 2009 opinion piece in the *Los Angeles Times* that stated the UN Intergovernmental Panel on Climate Change was pushing the idea of people abstaining from meat once a week. Rajendra Pancauri, chairman of that panel, argued that since meat production accounted for nearly a fifth of global greenhouse gas emissions, people might consider changing their eating habits and abstain.

As the *Times* reported, "a red-meat eater in a Prius is probably hurting the environment more than a vegan in a Hummer." As a result, the UN panel is pressing governments to launch campaigns to get diners to reduce their meat consumption. This has got to put a smile on the face of most Catholics my age who lived through that period of "meatless Fridays." It was a sin. The nuns at St. Thomas warned us hell would be our next home if we so much as daydreamed about a hamburger or ham and eggs.

On Fridays, we'd gather in the basement of the school and unwrap our salmon or tuna sandwiches. The stink from the fish was like damp socks.

Now and again, somebody would smuggle in a piece of chicken, and the bidding would start. This delinquent boy would wave a greasy chicken leg above his head. Suddenly we were all in a frenzy—kids bartering cupcakes, chocolate bars, pocket change, handfuls of baseball cards—anything to get that piece of meat. The last thing we cared about was hell. Besides, we knew were going to confession the next afternoon. The odds of us dying before that seemed on our side. Tomorrow, we'd line up along the aisles of Our Lady of Guadalupe, knowing we'd never be denied forgiveness and the price we paid would be four Our Fathers and three Hail Marys. Then we were in the clear, free as a bird, and pure as Ivory soap.

Fridays for Catholics were meatless. Our mothers doled out oven-baked fish sticks or fish cakes like punishment. Or canned spaghetti. No meat sauce. Or fried eggs.

Now and again, my father on his way home from the factory would swing by a hole-in-the-wall fish and chip place on Ottawa Street in Windsor. We'd hear the slap of the screen door at the back of the house and we'd run to greet him as he carried this bundle of fish and chips, all gathered in *Windsor Daily Star* newsprint. Those were the days hot lead was used in the printing process. Imagine that soaking into the fish.

Anyway, we'd scramble to the table, and fill our faces with fatty fish and chips. Such meatless Fridays were glorious. Years later, as a teenager, I'd wait up with my father past midnight and he'd dispatch me to a late night diner to fetch a couple of hotdogs smothered with mustard and onions.

So what's with that law where for centuries Catholics abstained from meat? Indeed, it was a papal decree introduced about eleven-hundred years ago by Pope Nicholas I, who declared eating of meat on that day was "a mortal sin." Of course, the nuns were quick to tell us that if we died in the state of "unrepented mortal sin" we were headed straight into the arms of Lucifer, so help you God!

The abstinence from meat had its roots in St. Paul's First and Second Epistles to the Corinthians. Pope Innocent III in the 13th century agreed with this. So did Pope Alexander. But at the Second Vatican Council, Pope Paul VI decided we didn't have to abstain from eating meat. With that, France, Canada, Mexico, Italy, and the U.S. opted out.

A housewife reacted to this change with surprise: "Now, suddenly, I find out it isn't a sin. That's hard to understand."

Another woman, this one from Canada, rightly questioned the ruling and said, "Maybe you can tell me—what are they going to do with all those people sent to hell for eating meat on Friday?'"

Good thing I didn't die in the 1950s.

Saint Joan

I WAS TOURING SOME VISITORS AROUND Windsor and landed up at the empty schoolyard of St. Thomas. This Catholic elementary school was shut down in 1991. Weeds poked out of the cement. I told these friends this was the neighbourhood in which I had grown up. I pointed out the house I grew up in on Prado, directly across the street. I told them about a woman who had resided in a house opposite it before the land was expropriated and the three-bedroom home was bulldozed by the school board to make way for expansion at the school. This was something the feisty Joan never agreed with and she didn't go down to defeat without a fight. That was in her nature.

The odd thing is that while my car idled on that concrete lot, Joan was dying at the Riverside Nursing Home. She passed away later that day. As I look back, I can only conclude that not everybody gets to have two mothers. Joan was my other mom. Well, I shouldn't be entirely possessive about this, because after all, she was a mom to the neighbourhood.

Let me be clear about this. Joan was nobody special that is, in terms of historical importance. She never ran for city council. She was never decorated in the war. Never won the lottery. Never saved anyone from near death. But to us she was a hero—a loquacious, mad, full of merriment mom. A woman who threw afternoon parties for the kids around Prado and Ontario Streets. A woman who rummaged through her closets for her husband's Second World War loot—Prussian knives, army medals, Nazi armbands—and dressed us all up as soldiers.

On hot afternoons in July, she'd ply us with Vernor's and popcorn and we'd hang on every word of those tall tales about Prohibition, her cousin, the eccentric, and enigmatic Art Reaume, former mayor of Windsor when good times were good, and when gambling was illegal but roaring in every Windsor poolroom.

Joan was also a crackerjack poker player and it was from her that we learned to play the game when most other kids were struggling with Go Fish, and Old Maid, and Crazy Eights. She coached us how to read a racing sheet and taught us the names of the great fillies that ran in the Kentucky Derby. And told us how her dog, "Dolly," was the offspring of a dog from Detroit's infamous Purple Gang. It was one of the many lies I wanted to believe.

Joan was a rare individual. She'd play a stack of 45s of Elvis, and Pat Boone, and the Everly Brothers and dance the *Chicken* with us in the afternoons. She was one of us. A mentor. A teacher. A friend. A mom who taught us the value of storytelling. A mom who could make you laugh, and make you feel deep emotion. She was Catholic and was raised by the nuns, but she stopped attending Mass years ago. She never said why, except maybe she was also raised by gangsters. And when she told me this, she'd bat her big eyelashes and smile, and swing out her hips.

In truth, it may have had something to do with her husband who had turned against the church. I never understood why. He had been an altar boy all through the war in Europe and served Mass for the army padres. Something changed his attitude, and when he died, he refused to have a priest give him last rites.

As kids we used to sit so still next to Joan on her back porch to watch the afternoon films hosted by the former actor Bill Kennedy. She'd lap up all the stories of the movie stars—all the gossip, dirt and glamour. Then enlarge on these for us, helping us live the lives of these heroes, and make us feel in our bones the wonder and mystery of the world around us.

Joan was special. I'm not sure if she ever kept the gift that was given to her by Hiram Walker years ago when she was interviewed by a British film company doing a documentary on rum-running for the company. They had filmed her because she was a child of the flapper age. The distillery gave her a gold-leafed bottle of Canadian Club with the inscription saying it was bottled for her. If there was any gesture to sum up her crazy nature it was this: Joan winking at the cameraman and telling him, "I never drank anything else!" They loved it.

It's true not everybody gets to have two mothers. Then again, not everybody gets to mourn two mothers.

Frank's: Language of The Street

I learned my first swear words at Frank's. Words for parts of the body I didn't know I had. Or thought I'd get someday soon. Or should. Or prayed I would.

Body language.

In that diner on Wyandotte men with floppy, wool caps ogled the nyloned curves on the legs of demure women from the Canadian Imperial Bank who came in for a coffee. That's when I heard those words. After the women left, the men would talk, guffaw, mutter things I never understood. My friend, Rocky, who lived with his grandmother above one of the stores on Wyandotte told me these were "bad words," or swear words. Once, I rode on the back of his bicycle at twilight in the summer and told him I didn't think such words were bad at all.

I was awed by such language. I'd retreat to the Legion across the street, and slump against a tree in the parking lot, and practice the words, I'd recite them hurriedly like the Our Fathers and Hail Marys. Silently. Defiantly.

After a while I'd try them out, ignorant of their meanings and let them fly into the wind at passersby. It was like flipping open the dictionary to invoke anything I stumbled upon, then catcalling and deriding anyone getting off the bus or coming out of the beer store, branding them all "stupid paleontologists!" or yelling at someone lurching out of the Legion how I couldn't tolerate their "onerous face" any longer. Meanings were irrelevant. Words gushed out of me as if I'd been given new power, new authority.

Then one late Sunday afternoon, my father overheard me

talking to a friend and using one of those words. I saw him coming. He crossed the street with purpose, and led me back to our house, and led me into the house, and took a bar of soap, and made me open my mouth, and he shoved it inside. Tears streamed down my cheeks. I couldn't focus. I couldn't really hear what he was telling me. But I knew I had crossed over into a region of language that wasn't acceptable.

Saturday I was at confession, obeying my father's wishes and telling the priest what words I had used. He asked me what they were, and I told him straight out—letting fly a colourful lexicon, mostly having to do with the body and God the Father. Father Mooney—silent for what seemed forever—told me such language would bar me from heaven. He said, "God blessed you with the ability to speak—you now have to find the right words to make yourself worthy of him."

Fighting The Cold War

It was the year the Braves had beaten the Yankees and that made us happy because everybody on this side of the river hated the Yankees. Everybody but us in the neighbourhood was ready for war. Down the street, families had already constructed bomb shelters. Others had stockpiled cans of beans and wieners, and Vernor's, and Heinz ketchup. Others stored vast amounts of canned water, first aid, dosimeter, and Geiger counter radiation measuring devices.

We on the other hand seemed to be the only ones in the neighbourhood oblivious to the Russians. Billy told me not to worry about them. He said if there was a war and they used the Bomb, we'd all end up with three heads and four tongues anyway after the radiation.

Naturally I became fixated with such a possibility, secretly hoping one of my heads would be able to figure out long division because the one I had wasn't any good.

That's when he told me about the secret weapon Catholics possessed. The rosary. It was the only thing capable of combating the Russians. There was no point in relying upon intercontinental ballistic missiles, or jet-powered interceptor aircraft or B-47s and B-52s. And when everyone else down the street—mostly the Protestants—were heeding the words of Joe McCarthy who was hunting down communists and perverts in every sector of society, we were on our knees praying the rosary.

We gathered nightly about the dining room, the radio humming, listening to Fulton Sheen clipping off hundreds of Hail Marys, Our Fathers, Glory Bees.

There we were: five brothers, my oldest sister, my mom and my dad, on our knees, all at war at 228 Prado Place in Riverside. Doing our bit.

Rocket Boys

I HAD FORGOTTEN ALL ABOUT IT until I went to see the movie *October Sky*, the story of the "Rocket Boys" who, inspired by the Russian Sputnik, created their own rocket ship. In 1957 we would scramble into my older brother's tarpaper shack that served as an observatory in a vacant lot on Prado. He had fashioned his own telescope, and we could examine craters on the moon.

But it was better to stand outside under the night sky and peer up at this Russian miracle, this satellite that sped faster than the imagination. Like so many others along that street who carried babies and guided children out to the schoolyard at St. Thomas, or stood on front porches, or beside their cars along the road, we gathered near our shack and watched this magical spectacle in wonder.

It wasn't long after that my older brother Bud started construction of his own rocket in my dad's garage. He cleared out the wire pigeon cages. He scrounged metal from a scrap yard, got use of a lathe down the street, and with the aid of various substances pilfered from the chemistry lab at what was then Corpus Christi (now Brennan High), and gunpowder supplied by a local Wyandotte Street pharmacist, Bud built this long thin tube of a rocket.

He made us hunt down field mice to find a suitable passenger to ride this rocket into the wild blue yonder.

"You see," Bud explained patiently, "This will be the first mouse to fly in outer space!" We were about ten or eleven. And listened in awe. We were also under threat of punishment if we leaked one word of this to our parents. My dad knew nothing about the experiment. He sat in the living room reading the paper. Or hugged the Zenith radio listening to the Friday night fights.

This was the Cold War. Fifties. A fridge cost 150 dollars; a TV, 300 dollars. We watched *The Price is Right, Queen For A Day*, and *Howdy Doody.*

Neighbourhood kids believed it would work. It's because of what I told them. I disclosed my dad's secret mission. The thing was, I was embarrassed every time a friend showed me the Iron Crosses, Nazi arm bands, and Adolph Hitler photographs their dads had carted back from German towns when they fought the Nazis. They'd ask what kind of loot my dad brought back. The truth wasn't sufficient. He was refused by the military on health grounds. He spent the war in a munitions factory. But I told my friends my dad had been a spy all through the war and worked at a factory now, but only as a cover to root out communists.

I also told them Ike still telephoned regularly. In the eyes of my friends that made my dad gigantic. They'd stroll past my house in dumbfounded silence and see him on the front verandah quaffing a beer and reading the paper like any ordinary man.

So it was plausible to the neighbourhood kids that we should scurry for mice for the rocket ship. Ike was behind it.

It wasn't until an early summer evening we got word the launch was that night. My dad and mom lounged on the front verandah. We raced up the basement steps, having been alerted that it was going to happen. Kids hurried from houses all over the neighbourhood to the empty lot beside our house.

There on a small flat launching pad, rested this silver rocket. It stood about three feet high. We gathered around it. I saw my mom leaning over the porch, and heard her calling, "What are you boys doing?"

"Nuthin'" came a quick chorus of boyish voices.

We watched Bud remove a tiny mouse trapped in his coat pocket. He slipped it smoothly into a tiny chamber, and shut the lid. He advised us to back up. We did. We stood alongside the lilac trees near the driveway. He set the switch then backed off. The fizzle stretched to an eternity then suddenly there was the explosion. The rocket burst into the twilight.

By now, my dad was racing down toward the lot. The rocket blasted over a neighbour's house across the street, and soared higher, and higher, then lightly plummeted like a wounded hawk, and fell on the roof of St. Thomas School.

In that instant, we became the Rocket Kids of Prado Place.

Marty Gervais

July Was Golden

July was golden.

A month when school has vanished from our thoughts.

A time when we woke to mornings full of sunlight with only thoughts of scrambling out of bed to a bowl of *Wheaties* and playing ball in the nearby lot.

And on that last day of school, thousands of kids bolted out of the front doors of elementary schools all over this land, leaping headlong into summer holidays, carrying ratty bunches of papers, broken three-ring binders, curled-at-the-corners, and daily journals that sometimes say more about what goes on in their houses than we all care to know.

And they leap straight into July, that golden period, that free month, that neutral zone of months when there's no thought of school, none of those newspaper August flyer-days with back-to-school advertisements, a month that belongs to youth.

I can't forget 1957. That summer I was ten. That last day of school in Riverside when the nuns, right to that last moment of the day, patrolled the aisles like Dobermans, struggling to keep us focused, occasionally "letting up," as they would say, and permitting us some "fun" by holding a class spelling bee. We groaned. Unfortunately for me, I groaned too loudly and she was all over me, asking me why. I told her the truth—I was bored and couldn't wait to get home. And then to push my point further, I spelled out the word in a smart-alecky manner: 'B-O-A-R-D!"

"Wrong!" the nun shot back.

"What?" I asked, not realizing I had misspelled the word.

That day when my buddies had filed out into the late afternoon, and home for the summer, I sat at my school desk and wrote the word out 150 times on foolscap. Sitting by myself writing out lines in the schoolroom under the glare of this sister. Then washing down the boards, and stacking up the school texts, and cleaning the brushes outside.

And then home. My report card tucked into my *Highroads Dictionary*.

A pass into grade seven with these words of advice: "Marty needs to pay more attention...He daydreams too much and talks too much..."

But I was free. Free for now.

And summer had begun and the days were already getting longer and that next night I joined my best buddy bound with his family for the Skyway Drive-in and we sat out in the humid summer evening leaning up against the chrome bumper of his brand new Pontiac to watch Yul Bryner in *The King and I*.

The sky was awash with stars. Nothing could be better than to be out of school. Nothing could be better than to sit in this moment, staying up late, savouring the nighttime.

The summer of '57. A stretch of days of Saturday matinees, watching Westerns. Or days filled with sandlot ball in the nearby schoolyard. Or riding the Tunnel Bus to Detroit to sit in the bleachers at Briggs Stadium to cheer the Tigers or catch Mickey Mantle at the plate.

We were kids. We thought of nothing important. Nothing about the space race, the Dodgers moving from Brooklyn to Los Angeles, the problem in the Suez, nor the election victory of John Diefenbaker in June.

None of this mattered. We were kids. We indulged ourselves. We danced the *Chicken* in the cool basements of our youth. We crowded into Baillie's Music store on Pelissier downtown and bought a 45 of Elvis Presley's *Loving You*.

Nothing could be better.

Street Level Glory

I had ninety-seven goals that season. Thirty-four assists. Dozens of game winners.

I had it all. I was eleven. I dominated the game. And so when my parents picked up stakes and moved to Bracebridge I was an instant hit because when I was asked how many goals I had scored my last season, I didn't hesitate for a second.

"Ninety-seven, give or take," I said nonchalantly.

Straightaway, without even trying out for the town's travel-hockey team, I was placed on the roster. The coach slapped me on the back and told me I didn't even need to dress for the practice.

"Not a ninety-goal scorer!" he announced to the dressing room, intentionally trying to intimidate everyone else.

Suddenly everybody wanted to be my friend.

The only problem with this perfect picture was that I had failed to tell them I had never been on skates in my whole life. I also neglected to say the ninety-seven goals I had garnered were from road hockey and even a few sprinkled in from table hockey games played with my brother. It didn't seem important.

Skating? I figured that would be a snap. I was pretty quick in my running shoes, so why should skates slow me down?

My first moment on steel blades in our first practice was falling flat on my butt in front of my teammates. It was discovered then and there that I couldn't skate. I was summarily banished from the travel team and scratched from all the grandiose plans of my hockey coach who had already penciled me in for the first line.

I spent the rest of my hockey days in house league, learning the painful experience of simply keeping up.

I tell this story because of the decision by town council in Rothesay, N.B., to outlaw road hockey on its streets. Bobby Orr came out in opposition of the new law, arguing that he and his friends honed their skills during the warm seasons scoring goals on makeshift nets on side streets and parking lots. He suggested the problem in kids' sports today is they're not going out and having that kind of fun with hockey.

Road hockey was a blast. And sure, I counted the goals. Why not? I was eleven. What do you expect? But like thousands and thousands of Canadian kids, I played from daylight to dusk. Played every afternoon after school with the only lights on the road emanating from nearby houses. Played until our pants were stiff from snow and ice. Never tiring of it. Never taking the time to go home for supper.

And while I might try to argue the case that this is what life was like in the '50s and '60s, it isn't really any different today. Kids—no matter what age—still embrace the purity of a good road hockey game. Don't believe me?

Once I had to drop off a hockey stick for one of my boys because Todd Warriner—then playing for the Windsor Spitfires, and later for the Vancouver Canucks—had found himself immersed in a game with a bunch of nine-year-old boys. He played for the sheer joy of it.

Or what about Mike Caruana, an old hockey buddy of that same son of mine, who for years organized neighbourhood road hockey tournaments on Parent Avenue? The winner would be hoisted up and do a lively victory jig with a big, old milk jug serving as the Stanley Cup.

This is hockey at the grassroots. It's what we're all about. We celebrate it. It's in our bones.

I watched my own boys running out the door to battle their hockey sticks with neighbourhood kids, or stood in awe as I heard them on the phone putting together a game with some Triple "A" hockey buddies. An afternoon game at Optimist Park. Within minutes, cars crowded the parking lot, and bigger kids—most in their teens—descended upon the place with sticks and gloves.

Afternoon road hockey.

Boyish voices and slapping sticks in warm spring air.

It's still happening. Hockey in the streets. It's the thing that defines generations of Canadian kids. It's in our blood. So why not count this? Moreover, why not count these minor triumphs at street level?

The Basics

I didn't learn much when it came to spelling or arithmetic or history when I went to St. Thomas. I struggled through grade school, worried sick over passing and getting the strap regularly. I learned very little.

I may have been able to rattle off the batting averages of every player on the Detroit Tigers. I may have been able to tell you the entire history of the Indian wars because I was fascinated with Davy Crockett. Of course, none of this was on the curriculum. None of this helped.

But I could paint pictures. If anything spared me from the wrath of the Sisters of St. Joseph, it was this ability to draw and paint. No one could paint a picture of the Holy Family better than I could. No one could portray Jesus on the Cross—dripping blood, and prickly thorns, and nails—as I did. It saved me. It elevated me to a higher status. I was special.

For years my parents cursed the school for having failed to teach me—or my brothers—the basics of reading, writing, and arithmetic. I didn't realize until much later how much I actually learned at the hands of this stern and judicial Sister Mary of Perpetual Help. I never realized how much she had opened my eyes to the possibilities of the imagination, to the significance of art.

She may have fallen down when it came to the basics, but on those beloved winter afternoons, she'd tell us to put away our books and she'd read us *The Silver Chalice* by Thomas Costain or *Huckleberry Finn* by Mark Twain. We would slump down in our desks—silent and lost in her words—enthralled with the stories that lifted right off the page that came alive in our hearts. When she would finish a chapter, we'd press her on to read more, and out the window went the exercises, the tests, and everything else we were supposed to be doing.

Instead we entered the world of the imagination, the world of literature, the eccentricities of language, and the magic of storytelling.

If we weren't doing that, the sister would order us to clean off our desks to make room for those large, textured watercolour sheets of paper for us paint.

Within minutes, the classroom was transformed into a veritable studio, as the sister strolled the aisles coaching us, reassuring us, sometimes leaning over and taking the brush from our hands to show us how to free ourselves, to embrace that fluid movement of a line. And from her brush would grow a face, a gesture, an expression.

When I learned that Lasalle-born Sister Mary of Perpetual Help (Nora Mary Dufour) had died in London, Ontario at ninety-three, I thought of the myriad of things that were wrong with the education system and still are. Many of us still count on our fingers. Many still don't know where Uruguay is. Or how to spell it. Yet Sister Mary—a legend among art educators who taught in Windsor's schools as well as at the Banff School of Fine Arts and whose own paintings still hang at the convent in London—was a mentor, an inspiration.

The boys and girls she taught know something of what it means to paint, what it means to hear a good tale, what it means to drink in the world and pay attention to what's going on around us. She taught us that. She taught us to see the world—and to respect it. That was enough to sustain us. That was enough to sustain whole generations of kids growing up with her.

That was enough.

Period.

Never Say Goodbye

THEY FINALLY TORE DOWN ST. THOMAS and the night before they started demolition, I drove by the place, turned off the engine of my car and sat there. It was twilight. I thought I should write a eulogy, one last goodbye.

Maybe for the last time.

I slumped in silence. Across the street was the house I grew up in. A place with a big wooden veranda that we would've burned down unintentionally if it weren't for a water hose being shoved through the slats and dousing the bonfire I believe my cousin Dennis had ignited underneath this structure. We were ten or eleven and scurried like rats out of there with my father wildly swinging a two-by-four at us as we dashed to freedom. All afternoon we feared our return home. Somehow late in the day, we succeeded in getting inside the school basement.

In the gloom, we played floor hockey, kicking blackboard brushes we used as pucks. We kept the lights off, managing entirely on the dim streetlights nearby and the remnants of daylight from the grated windows. We forgot all about the time. We forgot all about the sin of nearly burning down the house. We simply forgot. And we played—our voices echoing in the school basement as we replayed great moments from the NHL playoffs. We pretended to be the Rocket, or Gordie Howe or Marcel Pronovost or Andy Bathgate.

Then we heard our mothers calling us home. We imagined them standing outside our house on Prado, arms folded, and eyes searching frantically up and down the street. Our names ricocheted among neighbourhood homes. We finally slipped out a side door—our pockets bulging with rigid sticks of chalk pilfered from a supply room. One of my brothers justified that it was OK to take whatever we liked, because the school was really ours. It was part of our every day, a part of our growing up, our identity. Like the neighbourhood—we owned it.

There was some truth to that idea that I now understand. Certainly not the misappropriation part, but more that perception of tenure. There was a time in the '50s when we defended our neighbourhood, our school. Not in field days with coloured ribbons of first, second, and third. Not in organized sport. But in battles. Fist fights in the field lots nearby. Or on the scrubby baseball diamond at St. Thomas. Or in makeshift boxing rings my brothers rigged up across the street. One summer I was tossed into that ring, wearing a bathing suit for boxing trucks and facing a kid from St. Rose, two years older. No warning. No preparation. Just my brother Billy whispering into my ear before shoving me to the centre of the ring. "Hit him first!"

All I recall, when I spotted by brother departing the ring, I stupidly turned around, and suddenly was slammed in the back of the head. Knocked down. Knocked out. Then there appeared my brother's face—so large—looming over me. "What happened?" he was demanding. "What happened?" I couldn't speak. The rest of the week, I had to put up with my cousin Dennis harping about how I had somehow let down the neighbourhood, let down the school. He threatened to break my glasses again.

Back then, we believed in the neighbourhood. We owned it. We didn't join organized sport—we organized it ourselves. Baseball tournaments, road hockey games, boxing matches, poker games, marbles, and even sword fights with pine swords. We also set off rockets.

Everything revolved around that school. We were always in the schoolyard, or across the street in a vacant lot. We had no need of committees. No need for fundraisers. Or lawyers. Or parents. We made our own decisions. Took our own measures.

I'd say, if this were 1957 all over again, certainly we might've openly griped, and prayed for the school to be shut down forever. But if push came to shove, we would have never let this happen.

After all, this is where we grew up, where we were shaped, where we learned to cope, where we learned to be who we are today.

We'd never let this happen. We'd never say goodbye.

Two Boys in Riverside

We lived a block apart on Prado Place. We were in the same class at St. Thomas. We were boy scouts together. We played ball at the former Princess Elizabeth schoolyard. We served as altar boys for the stern Father Dill at Our Lady of Guadalupe when it was housed in that white-frame building that still stands at the back of the present church.

Fifty years later, we met for breakfast at Baker's on Wyandotte in the old neighbourhood. I was curious to learn something about my old buddy and wonder how it was that two Catholic boys, raised in the sandlots of Riverside and attending the same schools, could both wind up becoming authors.

Two boys a block apart.

I'm talking about myself and Eugene Moser, or "Gene" as I knew him. Two novels of his—both westerns—are on the market. Meanwhile, I've written a dozen or more books.

I stared across the table at this sixty-two-year-old man, and recognized that familiar broad face. As we talked, I realized we shared the belief that our childhood at Wyandotte and Prado helped shape our vision of the world, all those years of a Catholic education, and forking over fifteen cents for a matinee on Saturday afternoons at the Centre Theatre to watch John Wayne and Roy Rogers.

When I moved away, Gene stayed and went to high school. Life carried on for us. Marriage, kids, and jobs. Now this—trading stories of those long-forgotten years, before getting up and strolling down Prado to redraw the map of what our lives were like.

Instinctively, we pointed to houses and yards and tripped over our words as we tried to pin down shared childhood moments on this street. All the many stories. Like the one about the elderly woman, a widow, whose house was torn down at the foot of Prado, and how money was found stuffed in the walls.

Or the family whose father won the Irish Sweepstakes. Or the juvenile delinquent boy, who lived with his grandmother above the shops on Wyandotte, and tutored us in swear words, and later became a Detroit cop. Or the ice man who let us pluck broken chunks of ice off the end of his truck.

And what about Constantine's, a candy store on the next street where the aging owner shooed away the cats that skipped gingerly over the cardboard boxes of black balls, licorice, and bubble gum?

Or next door at the Esquire barbershop, where we read about the young up-and-comer Reno Bertoia of Windsor who was now playing with the Tigers. Or the well-thumbed pages of *Life* magazine that we pored over to study the photographs of the Cold War and Korea, or ogle the pictures of Marilyn Monroe.

Gene maintained the neighbourhood drew him back. After his first marriage failed, he moved back. Not really understanding why, he guessed it was as close to home as anything. And that's where life began for him, really. It defined him in those formative years. Now Gene resides in Stoney Point, and from there he writes, ever aware of the strong emotional tie to Riverside's streets. I heard it in his words.

"I still play ball," he said, remembering sandlot ball till dusk, till you couldn't see the ball anymore, all the while ignoring calls beckoning him home. Gene perfected the game, and was with the Riverside team in the mid-60s that captured the provincial championship.

When he retired, after working first in banks and later in factories, Gene turned to writing. "I had always talked about it," said Gene, but never seriously. But soon he was writing every day, and gravitated to producing the novel, *Six Gun Justice*, a story about a Texas Ranger who tracks down a notorious outlaw. The idea for it sprung from those Saturday afternoon westerns at the Centre. Gene's next book, *Lone Star Justice*, continues where *Six Gun Justice* left off.

And so there we were idling at the corner of Wyandotte and Prado, catching up. When we shook hands, Gene promised to send me a photograph of that day when we made our First Communion.

I can't forget that day. Father Dill was the celebrant. He was a stern pastor, a priest whose theology was black and white. Your choice—heaven or hell? Salvation or sin? He stood in the aisle at Our Lady of Guadalupe to talk to us one afternoon a week before we made our First Communion. He leveled with us. He told us the Devil made things look pretty good, and he could do anything for you, and give you anything you want, and he could gift-wrap for us the most spectacular present, but half way through opening it you'd realize this was a terrible bargain—you'd lose your immortal soul.

With God, it was a different matter, Father Dill said. God wasn't going to lift a finger to get you to heaven. It was up to you.

Make your own choice.

That intrigued me. I kept thinking about what I could get. I really wanted a new bike. I really wanted to pass. I really wanted to hit a home run on the ball diamond next to the school—simply to show the neighbourhood. I could have all of that, couldn't I? Or I could wait it out and go to heaven. Such thoughts scared me. It's a difficult choice when you're six.

But that day, a Sunday in late spring, I made my First Communion, and walked home with my mom. The lilacs were flowering. The sky above the storefronts in Riverside glistened from the rain the night before.

There was nothing better.

In that photograph, Gene is fifth from the left in the front row.

My forehead in the back row is all that you see of me—I am at centre of the picture. Brush cut and big ears. I'm not sure how Gene felt, but I thought it was the most perfect day of my life.

The Arena

It was at the end of summer in 1958 that my father pulled up stakes and moved north. Dief was the new prime minister. JFK was planning his run for the presidency. The recession was beginning to bloom. And my father had recently opened up a branch plant of the Windsor-based Canadian Motor Lamp and hired 150 in a town of 2,900. We had moved to a sprawling house on Manitoba Street, the town's main street. From the attic windows I could see the rounded roof of the Bracebridge Arena, a place where I'd spend both winters and summers.

In 2009, the old barn was celebrating its sixtieth anniversary and that summer, as with most, I trekked back north. I stepped inside the arena to show my sons where I had played house league hockey on Saturday mornings and where at night I watched the Bears trounce any team that lumbered through this winter town.

In the summers, the wrestlers—Happy Farmer Humphrey, Gene Kiniski, and Whipper Billy Watson—would strut up Manitoba like circus freaks to attract attention and lure fans to the matches in the old barn. As kids, we'd trail dutifully after these giants of the ring. I spotted one fighter pause at a gas station grip four or five bottles of Orange Crush in one hand like he was holding a bouquet of flowers, and then drain them all in one gulp. There was also the 750-pound Humphrey who had a 101-inch waist and wore polka-dotted tights and moved like a house up the main street's steep hill.

I was growled at by Whipper Billy Watson when I asked him to hand me back my dad's pen that he'd used to scrawl out his autograph. He had continued signing his name with it for other fans. I felt so hurt, I made a paper airplane of his autograph and sent it soaring into the arena seats.

In winter, the place was my second home. Nearly every night after school, I'd pack up my skates and head to the arena. I was also there every Saturday afternoon and back again at night to watch the Bears run away with yet another victory. I marvelled at Roger Crozier (later a Hall of Fame goalie) standing straight and tall in the net and casually watching the play like a farmer looking out over his ploughed field.

These were the glory years of the recession. As kids, we didn't even know what that meant. There was food on the table. New skates under the Christmas tree. Hot oatmeal in the mornings, and bacon and eggs on Sundays right after Mass. Gas was cheap. So were cigarettes. So were haircuts. Life was pretty good, despite the doom and gloom on the one television channel we got in that town that faithfully brought us Leafs games Saturday night, Ed Sullivan on Sundays, and Don Messer's Jubilee on Mondays.

The arena was the lifeblood of Bracebridge—the place of political rallies, Rotary Club raffles, auctions, religious revivals, lacrosse tournaments, air cadet marches, you name it. It's where we hung out.

That summer of 2009, I strolled through the empty

dressing rooms that are tucked under its sloped ceilings. I settled down on one of the old, wooden benches and summoned those years when we elbowed each other for space in these dreary quarters.

A moment that stands out for me is waking at dawn, long before everyone—I was in panic over having forgotten my new hockey gloves in one of those rooms. I tiptoed out of the house and made tracks in the new fallen snow to the arena where I was grateful to see a light on inside.

When I slipped through the unlocked door, and down to the dressing rooms, I heard clatter on the ice. That's when I spied Crozier, all geared up in net and someone I didn't recognize firing shots at this young goalie.

Years later, I would open the *Toronto* Star and see this same goalie making a name for himself in Detroit.

That image in that pre-dawn arena stands out for me. Here was a young man dreaming maybe of a moment in the not-so-distant future when the roar of places much larger than this would be deafening. But deep down he would always know that it started here. Maybe that morning.

Keep Your Mouth Shut

I WAS THE NEW KID AT SCHOOL. A different town. My family had recently moved to Muskoka. I had come from a Catholic school where the nuns taught me. Music was discouraged. School plays and concerts were non-existent.

Now I was in grade seven and was beginning to relax among new friends, and a brand new teacher who knew nothing of my history as a daydreamer, and being a poor student.

Each year, this spinster elementary school teacher, Minnie McCracken, who seemed not a day under one hundred to the grade sevens, but was probably thirty-seven, would dispatch her pupils to her spinster sister, Mae McCracken, the music teacher. She would then whip the grade sevens into shape to form a school choir.

So there I was—this new kid upstairs—elbow to elbow with my new friends and singing my heart out. I was feeling on top of the world. Especially when Mae would edge a little closer and cup her ear to get a better listen from me. My chest would swell with pride. I felt special. I felt I was in the zone.

Finally, she'd stop the choir and petition me to sing a few bars. I'd catch my breath and do just that. I gave it my best. And she'd nod.

This went on for most of a week. By now I was certain I was being picked to perform a solo. I raced home to tell my mom. I told my friends. I told the aging monsignor. I told them all it was only a matter of a few days before Mae would give me the nod. The only reason she was delaying was because she hadn't found the right piece for me to sing.

I didn't waste any time. I checked out a few that I might

sing. I scribbled them out in my Hilroy notebook and brought it to school. I considered songs like *We Gather Together* and *There's A Green Hill Far Away.*

But that day, I got the word. I was there in the morning, exercising my voice in the schoolyard, oblivious to anybody, my head swimming in glory.

"Gosh, I'm good," I mused.

Then my whole world collapsed. I was in the music room, filing into line with the others to sing when Mae summoned me: "Would you come here, please?" She handed me a piece of paper. It was folded up. "Take this to my Miss McCracken downstairs."

I wanted to open it because I knew she had written the name of the solo. Minnie read the note. "Did my sister tell you?" she asked.

"Well, no," I stammered, "I mean, she didn't tell me which piece I'll be singing at the Christmas show, but..."

At that point, Minnie sat me down and told me this: I couldn't carry a tune and I was the only one in the class who would be excluded from the choir.

Saint in Galoshes

There was a time when St. Patrick's Day was what the Catholic Church designated as a "Holy Day of Obligation." At least in Bracebridge, Ontario. It didn't matter if it didn't apply to the rest of Canada, which officially observed it simply as a "feast day." As long as Monsignor John O'Leary, the town's eighty-year-old pastor, was alive, it meant he intended each and every one of his Catholic flock would be in the seats at St. Joseph on that blustery 17th day of March.

No excuses accepted.

And so we went. We were there on St. Pat's Day under threat of hell and damnation. We'd crowd the pews because, as he told us, what was good for Ireland was good for his flock. And so we went. We heard him talk about his favourite saint, about Holy Mother Church in Ireland, and about real devotion (rolling the "r" in that Irish brogue) to the sacraments in the land where God's disciple walked.

I was frightened when I first met this Irish priest in 1958. I was turning twelve. I was the new kid in this tourist town.

"I expect to see you at Mass every morning at seven!" the monsignor roared to me in the church sacristy. "You'll be my altar boy!"

And so it went. I was immediately enlisted in his service. It would be a mortal sin if I failed him! He'd toss me to the Devil if I didn't show up.

The monsignor was a broad-shouldered man, and overweight, and he had trouble with his legs, and his feet would swell up, and he'd have to wear galoshes instead of shoes. He'd wear them at Mass. It didn't help his health either that he puffed on a cigar most of the time. Actually made us carry wooden matches in our pockets so we'd be ready to light his cigar right after Mass. And the priest ate like a lumberjack.

They called him "Dollar Bill" O'Leary, because in the summers he'd goad the tourists at Mass with this refrain: "I want to hear rustle in the plate today—not jingle!"

It wasn't uncommon for him to stop the Mass midstream and point out to the entire congregation that someone had just arrived. He'd swing around, his vestments swaying and he'd castigate the latecomer with: "Well, look at this! He's finally decided to show up. C'mon, we have a seat right up here for you!"

Or he'd berate the tourists who had come in from the lodges wearing Bermuda shorts: "Nice to have you here Sunday morning dressed in your Sunday finery—wearing a bathing suit!"

That was the gritty side of the man. But they loved him in Bracebridge. Without fanfare, he cared for his flock, often sending his housekeeper to poorer families with new shoes or clothing or groceries. Done without fanfare. Without notice. Often out of his own pocket.

The last time I saw the monsignor was the day he gave his last sermon. That typical fiery exhortation. The piercing blue eyes, and that lilting brogue, and Irish temper shaking the rafters. That day he was in full throttle, when suddenly, his eyes went glassy and his large body faltered. In that instant, he toppled over the altar steps, fell flat on his face and died. The place was silent. The galoshes on his feet looked ridiculous.

We knew then he was a saint.

Little Did I Know

There was hope for me.

Or so my parents thought when they drove me to Scollard Hall in North Bay, a hundred miles away to finish my high school education. I wasn't doing badly in school in Bracebridge, but they, instead, envisioned the Resurrectionist Fathers shaping me into adulthood. And so I went. To live with them. To learn from them. To be with them, day and night, attending early morning Mass, studying, and maybe becoming one of them. A Resurrectionist.

My first day I placed my clothes into a locker in my bedroom, hung up a blue blazer, and gray, wool uniform pants, folded away my shirts, and tucked a diary under my pillow. I was ready. Little did I know, it would all come apart so quickly, so completely. Little did I know.

The first conflict was meeting a girl at Demarco's coffee shop. The family that owned that popular hangout sent their kids to Scollard. Burgers and milkshakes there—anything but the spaghetti, fish sticks, chili, and bologna at Scollard. The second problem was going to confession after I had gone out with this girl. I knelt in the darkness of the confessional. I knew it was my math teacher. He knew me. I told him I truthfully was not sorry for having sex with my girlfriend.

He didn't seem that upset. He simply wanted to know what I meant by sex. *Were you petting?* Yes, Father. *Were you kissing her passionately?* Yes, Father. *Did you put your tongue into her mouth when you kissed her?* Yes, Father. *Did you touch her?* Touch her, Father? Well, yes, I was kissing her. *No, son, were you touching her impurely?* Yes, Father. *Did you fondle her breasts?*

Yes, Father. *Did you like it?* Yes, Father. *Of course you did.* Huh? Father? *Yes, of course you liked it. Sex is beautiful. Sex is something you want to do. You are a healthy Catholic boy, and healthy Catholic boys want to have sex. Don't you?* Yes, Father. *So you were touching that girl...I know why she would allow that. That's because she is a Protestant. Right?* Yes, Father, she is a Protestant, but she believes in God. *Sure, she does. She'll say anything to take your immortal soul. Right?* I don't know, Father. *Sure she would, but anyway, what thoughts did you have?* Thoughts, Father? I don't know what you mean. *I mean were you thinking of the last test I gave you in Algebra?* Huh? Father? *Ok, let's do this. You couldn't answer the simplest question on that test in November. Remember the question about a poultry farmer having only chickens and pigs, and when the manager of that poultry counted the heads of the stock in the farm, the number totaled up to two hundred. However, when the number of legs was counted, the number totaled up to 540. How many chickens were there in the farm?* I don't know, Father. I'm

PUBLIC SPEAKING AND DEBATING CLUB: SEATED: Alan Stillar, Stephen Ranoslay, Stephen Parker, Anthony Maisano. STANDING: Charles Gervais, Joseph Masciulli, Robert Mandeville, Tim Nelson, John Donovan, James Roy, Michael Barrett, Mr. P. Haefling, (Adviser).

sorry I got that wrong. *You got that wrong because you were thinking about sex. Right? You were thinking of fondling that girl's breasts. Right? You were thinking that your soul is worthless. Right? All you wanted was that girl. You certainly didn't care about algebra or ge-*

ography or history or...God. Right? No, Father, I guess I wasn't. *Well, no problem. You put a stop to this. A Catholic girl wouldn't do that. A Catholic girl cares for her soul when she cares enough for her body, which is a vessel of goodness, something to be raised higher for the greater good of marriage, and procreation, the place where sex is to reign, not in the back seat of a car, or in the park, or in the washrooms of a train...*Yes, Father. Yes. Yes. Yes. Yes.

My girlfriend went to high school in North Bay. She was Protestant. Her parents never attended church. She was

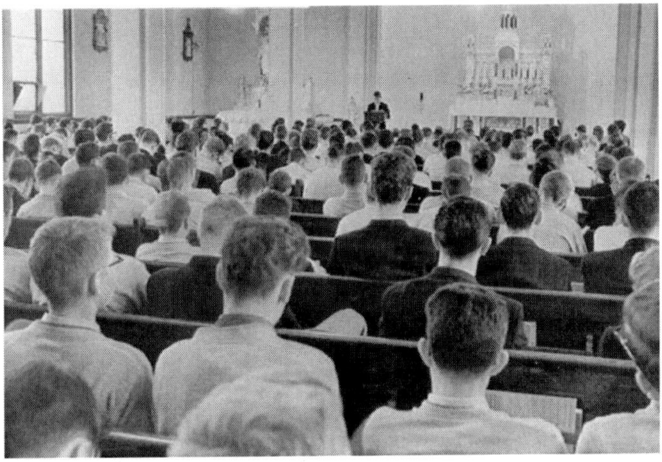

cute. I'd do anything to be with her. That's about the time I stopped dreaming of becoming a priest. I might as well have signed my death warrant for my soul. There was nothing I could do right.

• • •

We heard all sorts of tales as boarders. We didn't believe most. We heard that one of the priests challenged a senior student to a fight in the gym long after it was lights out, and there were mats flung on the floor, and the two slipped on gym shorts and wrestled. We were told another priest—livid with an Indian student—invaded his dormitory bed and beat him up. The student's face was bruised the next morning at Mass. We were told some boys made their way down the hallway late at night to speak to the priests about vocations, but also heard that *they* had become sacraments. We were told a lot of things, but refused to believe such rumours. These were holy men. They were our guardians. They were here to protect us.

• • •

Twenty-five boarders were suddenly handed out detentions, all at once.

We didn't know why. We hadn't misbehaved. We weren't failing. We hadn't mouthed off at the priests.

It took us a good day to figure it out—we all had girlfriends. Now we couldn't leave the building. Two-week detentions. By Thursday the punishment was lifted, but only if we went to the dance at St. Joseph's School, the boarding school for girls. We knew if we did this, our girlfriends would break up with us. Of course, the priests were counting on this. Their intention was to drive a wedge between us. We also understood if we didn't agree to date these St. Joseph students, we would

10-C: BACK (L-R) R.Jean-Marie, J.Gervais, F.Hains. B.Hart, J.Ursano B.Gonneau, R.Henderson, W.Moore, F.Shaw, T.Sawyer, A.Aistin, D.Henderson, R.Penrose, R.Campbell. CENTRE: (L-R) A.Briggs, R.Medley, G.Marrin, K.Atkinson, J.Hawn, D.Hillman, S.Reimer E.Edwards. FRONT: (L-R) L.Hollinworth, J.Duggan, E.Thompson, D.Rankin, M.Bryan, E.Woods, L.Hutton, K.Crockford, B. Middle-Brook.

never see the light of day. And so Saturday night we hopped into taxis and dutifully made our way to the front doors of St. Joseph's. We danced with the blind dates that were arranged by the priests and nuns. We couldn't believe our eyes when we witnessed the nuns circling the dance floor and sweeping in swiftly to ring tiny sleigh bells every time our chests neared the eager bosoms of these Catholic girls.

Sin was alive on the dance floor.

• • •

At Scollard, we were allowed to stay out Friday and Saturday nights until midnight. If we moseyed in one second after midnight, we faced a two-week detention. One night, I scrambled off the couch at my girlfriend's place—I was nearing that moment I had spent a entire semester trying to achieve when I realized I was going to be late, so I leapt to my feet, threw on my winter coat, and with my heart thumping in my chest, I raced across that football field to the front doors of the school.

The disciplinarian, who I would encounter years later in Rome, was standing at the top of the stairs tapping his watch. I arrived a minute after midnight. I was done. Two weeks of house arrest. I might as well have risked the sin. *Mine eyes have seen the glory!* Or nearly. And now I'd have to start all over again.

• • •

My last year at Scollard was the year that JFK was assassinated. It was also the year the bilingualism and biculturalism commission toured the country, and I rose to my feet at a rally in Sudbury and spoke and received a standing ovation. That same year Peter Newman wrote Dief's biography, and the flag debate started in earnest. I won the public speaking contest that winter, and ran away from that school a few times, and nearly blew up the chemistry lab. I broke up with my girlfriend that spring, and decided once and for all, I'd never become a priest. Not ever.

They weren't the kind of people you could trust.

Gone.

I crept along the main street in my car and saw that everything had changed in this town of my youth. The faces—once so recognizable at the post office in the morning or at the coffee shops—have long ago disappeared.

As I glanced around, I noticed the same old storefronts,

but now occupied by new businesses. Gone is the bakery near the falls with its fresh bread and sticky buns.

Gone is the barbershop on the slope of the hill on the main street that once belonged to a British-born oil painter who fashioned landscapes that he only imagined existed on the outskirts of the town.

Gone is the druggist who was reputed to have ventured into Algonquin with his mentor Tom Thompson to paint those deep lakes, blanketed with the colours of fall and burning sunsets on the wooden backs of cigar boxes.

Gone is the Parkview Diner next door to where former Ontario premier Frank Miller once sold used cars. Gone is the librarian at the stately Carnegie Library who told me I'd never be a writer unless I read everything by Emily Dickinson, Ernest Hemingway, and Plato.

Gone, too, is the original St. Joseph's where Monsignor John O'Leary died of a heart attack on the steps of the altar one Sunday morning in the middle of one of those hell-and-damnation sermons.

Gone is the dairy where I helped my brother load those heavy wooden crates of milk bottles and then ride with him in those open-air trucks to the lodges.

Gone is the tiny house across the street where the Crozier family lived, and where it was not uncommon to spot Roger—later an NHL hall-of-famer goalie—drag his equipment bag down the street to the arena.

When I returned there one summer weekend, I drove north to check out the town where I had grown up. The town then was "dry," which meant my dad had to drive to Gravenhurst to get a drink unless he joined the men at the Shell station who gathered in a back room at night to play poker, and drink and, smoke fat stogies under a dim light bulb.

At twelve, my buddies and I would clamber up on those dirty used truck tires to peek through the grimy windows and strain to hear what these men were talking about, knowing most of it was about women in the town and we were always feared we might hear our mothers' names mentioned.

After awhile, the men inside would hear us, and they'd swing open a side door, and startle us, and trail us down the alley. I'm sure these men are all gone now.

As I made my way through the town, I was hoping for some familiar faces, but I saw none.

The Norwood Theatre remains with its touches of art deco design in subtle evidence on its doors and ticket booth. The original Post Office with its towering clock tower continues to dominate the street. One summer, a prankster scrambled up inside the tower, and in the midst of a storm started frantically spinning the hands of the clock.

On my tour, I also stopped in at the Bracebridge Arena to check out the team photographs of the Bears when it was a senior "A" team in the glory years of the '50s and '60s. My brother, Bill, played right wing for them but never saw much ice time until Crozier got injured. That night, the coach surveyed the bench, and shouted, "Gervais, get the equipment on!" And Bill hustled into the dressing room, and emerged moments later decked out in Crozier's damp equipment. He was ready for action.

Ten minutes later, my brother was sprawled on the ice, his nose gushing with blood from a slapshot from the blue line. Those were the days when goalies wore no masks.

If you cut between the houses directly opposite that arena, you would emerge onto Manitoba and be standing in front of the house I lived in. The place is still there. A travel business now. From those tiny attic windows, I could appraise the town. I could see all the way to the Post Office, and spy the men and women greeting one another in the mornings. I could almost hear the monsignor shutting the door of the rectory at St. Joseph's and see him waddle his way up the main street, past St. Thomas's Anglican Church. I could see his cassock swaying as he marched past the town's businessmen. They ignored him. He was Catholic. They were Masons. I could see the man from my father's plant picking up the mail. I could see the Greyhound Bus arriving right on time en route to North Bay.

Which brings me to that crazy Saturday morning that I will never forget from my childhood. I was by myself in the attic, wondering about a radio play I had heard. The story was about a shoemaker who is approached by the Devil to play a game of curling. The man agrees but when he ventures on to the Devil's rink, he finds Macbeth, Judas Iscariot, and Guy Fawkes. I thought it was funny, but I was intrigued with the idea of a man selling his soul to the Devil. I wasn't sure I even believed in such things.

And so there I was, back then on that morning of my childhood, pacing the upper floor of our house. I could hear my mother preparing breakfast downstairs. I thought there has to be some way of proving there was a devil. I mean when most wrangled over the existence of God, I worried myself sick over whether there was Lucifer. Odd. But I had figured Gordie Howe had made such a Faustian bargain. In his first season with the Detroit Red Wings, he scored a measly seven goals in fifty-eight games. He didn't do all that much better the next two years then suddenly he exploded in 1950-51 with forty-three goals. No rhyme or reason. I figured Winston Churchill had. Maybe Hitler. I wouldn't have put money on those two rising so fast to the top.

But who could be sure?

So I paused at the attic window. I was twelve. What did I know?

"Go ahead! Take my soul!" I whispered.

Nothing happened. The sky didn't darken. The trees didn't topple over. The roof didn't peal back. And my mom was still calling me downstairs for breakfast as she always had, and it tasted exactly the same.

Nothing.

Then I thought, oh, that's dumb—what if I gave away my immortal soul for nothing? I mean I didn't really make a bargain. I just gave it away like an old baseball mitt I no longer needed.

Then I forgot about it. Life went on.

But in the coming weeks, my mother marveled at how I had finally turned things around at school, and I was passing grade seven with flying colours. I panicked. I thought, I gave up my soul to pass grade seven? C'mon! That's not fair.

As I say, I was reflecting about all this as I ambled down the main street many years later when I casually glanced up at the attic window of my old house. I swear for a second I spotted the curtains move slightly, and someone stir in the darkness.

Marty Gervais

Meeting The Devil

I WAS ON MY WAY TO ROME in the mid-80s when a Catholic bishop from the London Diocese suggested I might save some money if I bunked in with some priests he knew. They resided around the corner from the Spanish Steps. I took him up on the offer, and let him make the arrangements. I showed up late one morning after my flight from Toronto. Rang the bell at the street entrance and stepped inside.

Within minutes, a jovial priest took me to a room upstairs and handed me a card that provided background on their religious order. These were the Resurrectionist Fathers. I smiled. I knew them, of course. And the goodly priest detected my bemusement and inquired if I was familiar with their religious order. I confessed that I had gone to Scollard, the North Bay boarding school in the 1960s.

The priest looked surprised, and then remarked, "Isn't that coincidental! We have a priest here who taught at that school."

Well, over the lengthy history of Scollard Hall, there had to be a hundred priests who served as teachers. That's when this cheerful priest told me who it was. Apparently the prelate was there in Rome to assist in re-writing the order's constitution. In that instant, my heart stopped beating. He had been the disciplinarian. I had run afoul of him when I was fifteen. I had been in and out of his dim and cramped office at the end of the polished hall after hours of desperately perjuring my way out of some minor infraction. He wore Buddy Holly glasses. He was tall, lean, and swaggered whenever he roamed the floors. He was quick to punish. I'm not sure if he was terribly menacing. He was the only priest whose homilies on Sundays made any sense. But he was sinister in the way he would form questions.

My heart was dead in my chest. I hadn't heard or muttered his name since I was a teenager. Now I was a grown man, married, children, job, a mortgage, and a life well beyond Scollard.

The priest never noticed my consternation. He invited me to join him for lunch. A half hour later, I made my way to the refectory and was directed to a seat directly across from a graying man. I recognized him instantly. He greeted me and opened up with the questions immediately. This friendly exchange soon turned to a cross-examination.

"I was told you went to Scollard?" he said.

"Yes."

"You were there about 1963 or 1964?"

"Yes," I said, failing to elaborate.

"Boarder?"

"Yes."

"I don't recognize the name, the name 'Marty.' I knew a 'Charles,' but not a Marty."

My first name is Charles, and when I lived at Scollard, that was the name I went by, maybe because no one bothered to inquire as to what my family or my friends called me. Marty was a nickname that developed later. Even my parents didn't call me Charles.

I stared at this priest. I was no longer in my thirties. I was fifteen again. I was lying again when I told him, "I have no idea who Charles is."

He sensed my deceit, and refused to let that go.

"Really? I find it hard to believe that there would be two people with the same last name, both boarders, and both living there at that same time, and they wouldn't know each other."

True enough. That made sense. But I was lying. I didn't know why. I didn't know why this cleric had me in his grip. I wanted to run away, as I had done a few times when I was at Scollard. I slipped out of the school one afternoon, and hitched a ride to Mattawa, then turned around, and went back. I arrived late at night, and the disciplinarian was waiting for me. He was actually kind enough to let me return to my room and get some sleep, but I would pay for it with a lengthy detention.

But here I was in Rome, and he now had me in his hold. I was no longer an adult. I was under questioning, and what had I done wrong? What had I done to deserve this? Why did I lie? Why didn't I simply spit out that this was evidence of what that school had done to me?

Life as a Catholic had been sweet when I was much younger. We wanted to be priests. We wanted to be closer to God, to embrace all that purity and grace. We wanted truth.

I remember being a boy of eight and kneeling on the linoleum floor of my upstairs bedroom. I was on one side of the bed; my brother, Bill, on the other. The two of us knelt under a bare-light bulb that dangled from the ceiling. A wooden cross high above our pillows. We felt holy. We knew if we died that night, we were going to heaven.

Whatever happened?